# Fixing Broken Britain?

# Fixing Broken Britain?

## An audit of working-age welfare reform since 2010

Frank Field and Andrew Forsey

CIVITAS

First Published January 2016

© Civitas 2016
55 Tufton Street
London SW1P 3QL

email: books@civitas.org.uk

ISBN 978-1-906837-76-1

Independence: Civitas: Institute for the Study of Civil Society is a registered educational charity (No. 1085494) and a company limited by guarantee (No. 04023541). Civitas is financed from a variety of private sources to avoid over-reliance on any single or small group of donors.

All publications are independently refereed. All the Institute's publications seek to further its objective of promoting the advancement of learning. The views expressed are those of the authors, not of the Institute, as is responsibility for data and content.

Designed and typeset by
lukejefford.com

Printed in Great Britain by
4edge Limited, Essex

# Contents

# Authors

**Frank Field** has served as Member of Parliament for Birkenhead since 1979. In 1990 he took up the chairmanship of the Social Security Select Committee and continued in this role up to 1997. In that year he accepted the position of Minister for Welfare Reform in Tony Blair's first government. He then served as a member of the Public Accounts Committee between 2002 and 2005. In 2010 he was appointed by David Cameron to lead the Independent Review on Poverty and Life Chances. Frank co-chaired last year's All-Party Parliamentary Inquiry into Hunger in the United Kingdom and he currently chairs the Work and Pensions Select Committee.

**Andrew Forsey** is head of Frank Field's parliamentary office, having joined in 2013. In 2014 he served as Secretary to the All-Party Parliamentary Inquiry into Hunger in the United Kingdom. Andrew then wrote the inquiry's two follow-up reports in 2015, focusing on the extent and causes of hunger in this country.

# Introduction

## i. A second and third front in welfare reform

There is an urgent need to open up simultaneously both a second and third front in welfare reform. The thorny issue of dependency on benefits has bedevilled the welfare state since the 1970s and it has grown in importance in each of the past five decades. But the debate on dependency has been narrowly pitched in terms of the numbers of working-age claimants (aged between 16 and 64) drawing benefit for very long periods of time. No adequate distinction has been drawn between those in and out of work who depend on benefit. Nor has sufficient consideration been given to the dependency of employers and landlords who have drawn wage and rent subsidies from taxpayers that have grown exponentially.

The welfare-to-work strategy of successive governments since 1997 has begun to crack the dependency on out-of-work benefits that had appeared to be an almost intractable problem. We refer to this strategy as 'Welfare Reform Mark One'. Its success can be seen in the number of households with nobody in work falling in 2014 to its lowest level since 1996. Very large numbers of single mothers and long-term unemployed have moved into work. In 1996, almost 52% of households headed by a single parent were workless; in 2014 the figure stood at 33%.[1] An active welfare-to-work strategy has also ensured that other claimants moving on to the welfare rolls for the first time have drawn benefit for only a short period. The average duration of a Jobseeker's Allowance claim in 1996 never fell below 30 weeks. When the Labour government left office in 2010 this had been cut to 19 weeks. In October 2014, four and a half years into the Conservative-Liberal Democrat Coalition government, the average duration stood at 21 weeks. Moreover, on the eve of Labour's election victory in 1997, 54% of claimants drew benefit for more than six months. Thirteen years later this had fallen to 40% and, despite the fallout from the great recession, this figure since 2010 has not risen back above 50%.

The Coalition government's welfare-to-work programme, maintained by the majority Conservative government which prevailed at the 2015 general election, has continued the success of the previous Labour government in overall terms, albeit at half the cost. However, this success is not evenly matched among different groups of claimants. Claimants with disabilities and those aged over 50, for example, face particular difficulties in landing a job and the current welfare-to-work programme does little to equalise their job opportunities with others on the welfare rolls.

While much of the heavy lifting in helping claimants back into work has been accomplished, further work is necessary and the task now requires different skills from a traditional welfare reformer. A range of niche programmes needs to be developed for those who still face too high a barrier to entering work. The aim must be to extend the success that is already registering in welfare-to-work policies to those claimants with special difficulties that hinder their chances of successfully making this transition into work. Developing these programmes we have entitled 'Welfare Reform Mark Two'. Although refining the welfare-to-work programme in favour of the least advantaged remains of great importance, such a refining is now only a part of the agenda for welfare reformers.

The efforts of welfare reformers also need to be focused on a welfare-to-work strategy that not only moves claimants off out-of-work benefit, but more importantly helps them move up the pay ladder and out of poverty. This is the third welfare reform front, or 'Welfare Reform Mark Three', which needs to be opened up in the welfare-to-work strategy and robustly put into operation. This takes welfare reform into new territory and will require the best reformers' talents in the Department for Business, Innovation and Skills, as well as those civil servants at the Department for Work and Pensions – both in Whitehall as well as at a local office level – who have shown the skills necessary to develop welfare reform programmes. For the reverse side of the success in moving claimants from out-of-work benefit into work has been to switch the bill taxpayers meet from, say, Jobseeker's Allowance payments to footing the bill for tax credits.[2] Too many people on low benefit incomes have been encouraged into low-paid jobs whose rewards are only brought up to a more acceptable income level by the wage subsidy that sails under the colours of tax credits. At its peak in 2011 the bill for this wage subsidy – consisting of Working and Child Tax Credits – had reached £30 billion.

Welfare Reform Mark Three therefore must begin a programme of so helping raise productivity in lower paying firms that higher wages become affordable without creating unemployment. Such a programme becomes doubly necessary as employers move towards paying the government's new National Living Wage and then onto a more substantial voluntary living wage.[3] The first moves on how this could be achieved over the life of this parliament are outlined in the concluding section of this audit. What needs to be noted here, however, is that this strategy links Welfare Reform Mark Three into the key wider economic and political debate that now needs to engross the country more generally on raising productivity in British industry. It is only by productivity increases that real living standards can rise generally over the longer term for the whole population, although of course productivity increases on their own won't necessarily ensure that these rewards are fairly shared.

Previous recessions have always been followed by recoveries that signalled the rise in output per hour worked or, for short, increases in productivity. That productivity increase has failed to materialise since the great recession of 2008-09, although it is possible that the very first signs of the old order re-establishing itself are becoming visible. Why productivity has stalled is not the easiest question to answer. Part of that answer, however, must surely be that, for the first time, the British economy is being fed by what appears to be an almost never-ending stream of cheap labour, particularly from eastern Europe.[4]

Employers, faced with a new, eager to work pool of recruits, have appeared to settle on adding labour units to the existing capital stock, rather than using labour as a scarce resource and raising the capital mix so that output would rise without commensurate increases in employment.

With the wages of the low paid becalmed by this very significant increase in labour supply we suggest here that Welfare Reform Mark Three should open up a new front to ensure that those workers parked in low-paying occupations are able to increase their productivity and thereby move wage rates generally up towards the government's new National Living Wage and then onto a higher, substantial and sustainable living wage level.

It is noticeable that since the introduction of the statutory National Minimum Wage[5] the bunching of wages at and just a little above this base level would suggest that employers are viewing it not only as a minimum floor but an acceptable ceiling for their lower-paid employees' pay. Our belief is that by resolutely building on its introduction of a National Living Wage the government would not only cut significantly still further the tax credit bill, but could simultaneously kick-start the macro strategy of more generally raising the productivity of British industry.

## ii. The outline

This audit of welfare reform for working-age claimants since 2010 begins in Chapter 1 with a review of the impact the Centre for Social Justice has had in shaping part of the first front in welfare reform – incentivising work as the best route out of poverty.

Chapter 2 audits the outcome since 2010 of the government nailing its colours to a strategy of getting Britain back to work, before Chapter 3 audits the government's greater emphasis on making welfare conditional on claimants fulfilling certain duties to prepare themselves for the world of work.

How some of the government's policies made more difficult the task of enshrining work as the best route out of poverty is examined in Chapter 4, when the audit looks at those moves that have raised the bar to making work preferable to a life on benefit.

Auditing the numbers of working poor is the subject of Chapter 5, while Chapter 6 examines the progress the government has made in what was originally billed as the key welfare reform in fixing 'broken Britain' – Universal Credit.

The discussion in Chapter 7 then moves onto auditing how effective the government has been in reforming Incapacity Benefit and replacing Disability Living Allowance with Personal Independence Payment.

In bringing this audit to a conclusion we consider in Chapter 8 what we regard as the two clear successes of the government's welfare reform strategy since 2010. The first has been to achieve what no other government in the post-war period has ever achieved; namely, a cut in the working-age welfare budget (including tax credits), not simply as a proportion of total national income, but in real terms. Accompanying this success has been the emphasis – hardly spoken about and almost never reported upon – on strengthening families.

The audit closes with a stock-taking exercise, setting out what progress the government has made so far and how much is left to achieve, and pointing the way to the future of welfare reform during the 2015 parliament.

# 1

## 'Broken Britain': Relieving poverty by entrenching it

### i. The Centre for Social Justice blueprint

The ideas and programmes developed by the Centre for Social Justice (CSJ) after it was set up by Iain Duncan Smith in 2004 are crucial to understanding the government's welfare reform programme since 2010. When Duncan Smith was appointed work and pensions secretary in the Coalition he took with him into government not only the CSJ's executive director, Philippa Stroud, as his new special adviser, but also the think tank's assumptions and policy ideas about 'broken Britain'. These were laid out in a series of reports, beginning in 2006 with 'Breakdown Britain' and ending in 2009 with 'Breakthrough Britain', which set out how the welfare state was relieving poverty only by entrenching it.

In its 2009 report the CSJ proclaimed in the first sentence on the first page that 'our benefits system is broken'.[1] While the welfare state 'alleviates' financial hardship, 'it does so at a price'. This first page of the report then set out what the CSJ believed that price to be, namely, the 'high benefit withdrawal rates [that] trap millions in worklessness and dependency... often over several generations'. The CSJ diagnosis was that the rates at which benefits were clawed back as households either found work, or put in more hours, were enough to repel people on benefit from striving for their keep.

'Breakthrough Britain' was equally clear on how to put 'broken Britain' back together again. To address Britain's unacceptable levels of poverty and social exclusion, 'we need to redesign the benefits system and boost employment and earnings over the long term'.[2] Reinforcing this central assumption, the report added, 'this will require a new approach: one that recognises how claimants respond to withdrawal rates [of benefits]'. The prescription offered by the CSJ was to replace the current medley of means-tested benefits with a single means-tested benefit, called Universal Credit.

A note of warning needs to be sounded at the outset on Universal Credit, the mechanism through which the CSJ and Duncan Smith saw their welfare revolution operating.[3] The test of Universal Credit's success couldn't be more clearly defined by its architects: low rates of benefit withdrawal to incentivise work. We should not fall though for some of the propaganda surrounding the hesitant launch of Universal Credit. At the outset there was the obligatory reference to the reforms being the most significant since William Beveridge's plan for a comprehensive system of National Insurance and National Assistance. Such claims are regularly made by governments introducing their welfare reform programme. It was Tony Blair's claim for the 1997 Labour government's first green paper on welfare reform.[4] But the comparison is false; the rollout of Beveridge's plans and Universal Credit differ fundamentally.

The Beveridge scheme was put into operation through two acts of parliament, the 1946 National Insurance Act and the 1948 National Assistance Act, both of which were brought into operation on a single day. While Beveridge's scheme built on the existing structure of benefits to a degree that was perhaps not that well appreciated at the time, a totally new scheme came into operation on the vesting day listed in each piece of legislation.

Not so with Universal Credit. A totally new scheme began very tentatively in 2013, but the whole of the existing structure of benefits about which the CSJ is so rightly critical, continues to operate today. The principles underlying the CSJ's welfare reform programme were however not confined to Universal Credit. They were to be progressively applied to the existing welfare state. We therefore need to examine how well this welfare reform programme interlinks with existing schemes across the whole domain of benefits for families and individuals below retirement age. This is distinct from the success or otherwise of Universal Credit.

We also pose the crucial question in this audit of how well the government's welfare reform programme is achieving the objective of ensuring claimants are always better off in work than on out-of-work benefit, billed as the be-all and end-all of the reform agenda. But first, how were the commitments to welfare reform for working-age claimants fashioned in the manifestos of the two parties that set off down this path in 2010 and how did the making of the government's programme affect what was to become an agreed welfare reform strategy?

## ii. What the Conservative and Liberal Democrat manifestos said in 2010

The CSJ's analysis and its prescription, Universal Credit, were not reflected in the Conservative Party's 2010 manifesto. The manifesto, in its single page covering welfare reform, pledged to reduce the tidal wave of workless households, and with it the ratio of one in six children living in workless households – the highest in Europe – by getting people back into work. The prospect of 'ensuring everyone benefits from economic growth' was central to the party's means of achieving Labour's pledge of eliminating child poverty by 2020.

A promise was made to scrap Labour's 'failing' welfare-to-work schemes and so open the way to a single welfare-to-work programme. The manifesto then pledged support for small businesses, improvements to skills and a strengthening of higher education. Only in its section titled 'Make Britain The Most Family Friendly Country in Europe' did the Conservatives make any specific pledges on reforming the tax and benefit system. The manifesto was clear about ending the marriage penalty, whereby current rules ensure that couples on welfare who split up become financially better off. Significantly, the manifesto went on to pledge support for the tax credit system while withdrawing help from higher-income households.[5] There was no hint, let alone a specific pledge, to introduce the welfare reform programme that sails under the banner of Universal Credit.

The manifesto highlighted, in its section 'Get Britain Working Again', that a future Conservative government would aim to 'reduce youth unemployment and reduce the number of children in workless households'.

The Liberal Democrats' manifesto commitments were even briefer and centred on tax credits, which would be restricted. Scant details were provided of other benefit reforms and there was certainly no mention of any attempt to abolish much of the existing system by introducing Universal Credit.

## iii. The Coalition's programme for government

When the 2010 election resulted in a hung parliament our most senior civil servants arranged for coalition negotiations to take place behind closed doors. In a neutering of the doctrine of the mandate (whereby voters decide the main activities of a winning party's agenda) it was the negotiators who decided what was to become the winning side's manifesto. Voters were excluded from any knowledge of what bargains were being struck.[6] The first the public knew of what was left of the contents of the manifesto of the party for whom they voted was when 'The Coalition: our programme for government' was published 14 days after the general election. What did this document make of the welfare reforms the Conservatives and Liberal Democrats had explicitly pledged themselves to in each of their election manifestos?

The answer is very little. While more detail was given of reforms to Labour's welfare-to-work programmes, there was still no mention of what would later be claimed as the welfare revolution of Universal Credit. There was, however, one cryptic phrase at the very end of the 'Jobs and Welfare' section of the document, as if it was an afterthought, to the effect that the government would 'investigate how to simplify the benefit system in order to improve incentives to work'.[7] Manifesto watchers should have been on their guard. Labour had used a similar Delphic phrase in its manifesto for the 1997 election, heralding the tax credit system by pledging to 'examine the interaction of the tax and benefits systems so that they can be streamlined and modernised, so as to fulfil our objectives of promoting work incentives, reducing poverty and welfare dependency'.[8]

How these proposals for Universal Credit became the cornerstone of the government's welfare reform programme is a story that others will tell when the record of the 2010 parliament is written. Our aim is different. It is to conduct an audit of the consequences of the government's welfare revolution and its impact on reducing poverty and welfare dependency amongst claimants of working age, particularly by improving the incentive to work.

# 2

# Has the government managed to 'Get Britain Working' again?

## i. Work and welfare

Brief as the jobs and welfare section was in 'The Coalition: our programme for government', what was printed was highly significant. Eleven of the 12 proposals listed were built around the belief that jobs are the only effective route out of poverty and that government programmes should have this as their overriding objective. In the order they were listed, the government promised:

- A single welfare-to-work programme would replace Labour's spread of welfare-to-work initiatives;

- Claimants facing the most significant barriers to work would go onto the single welfare-to-work programme immediately;

- All claimants aged under 25 would be put on the welfare-to-work programme after a maximum of six months;

- Those organisations contracted to deliver the welfare-to-work programme would be paid on the basis of helping claimants into work;

- Welfare-to-work programme fees would be greater the longer the claimant remained in work;

- The receipt of benefit would be made more conditional so that those able to work would gain benefit only having demonstrated their willingness to work;

- The National Minimum Wage would be viewed as a protection for low-paid workers as well as an incentive for them to take work;

- All Incapacity Benefit claimants would be reviewed, with those fully capable of work being transferred onto Jobseeker's Allowance;

- Entrepreneurs would be supported to work for themselves;

- A range of service academies would offer pre-employment training and work placements; and

- A spread of work clubs would help develop and exchange the skills of claimants while offering mutual support.

How successful was the government in reducing the vast and growing working-age welfare bill – which had grown in real terms from £64 billion in 1997 to £96 billion in 2010 – by ensuring those claimants able to work were helped to do so?

## ii. A single welfare-to-work programme

The heavy lifting of ensuring that claimants moved into work was assigned to the new single welfare-to-work programme, known simply as the Work Programme, although it was not yet named as such in the Coalition's programme for government. The government committed itself to sweeping away 'all existing welfare-to-work programmes [to] create a single welfare-to-work programme so as to help all unemployed people to get back into work'.

While a criticism of the Work Programme as it turned out could be that it was designed to be a one-size-fits-all model, its importance has been in its innovatory payment system, based not simply on placing the unemployed into work but weighting payments more heavily towards help for those most difficult to place in a job. The Work Programme had commitments on this score which were to create a payment-by-results system so that the income of those organisations contracted to deliver the programme would reflect more closely their success in getting all groups of claimants into work. Further reform of the funding formula was promised so that providers were more generously rewarded the longer they helped claimants remain in work.

The government made clear at the outset that Jobseeker's Allowance claimants who faced the most significant barriers to work were to be referred to the new welfare-to-work programme immediately, and not after 12 months on benefit, as was the case under Labour's main programme, the Flexible New Deal. Furthermore, Jobseeker's Allowance claimants aged under 25 would be referred to the Work Programme after a maximum of six months on benefit.

Events showed that it was more challenging to meet the commitments which had been expressed so simply and clearly at the outset. Once operational, and only months after signing the Coalition commitment on welfare reform, the government began backtracking. It announced changes to the Work Programme so that those aged 18-24 would join only after nine months on Jobseeker's Allowance, rather than after six months as had been promised.

Claimants referred to the Work Programme were to be assigned to contractors, whose job was to help them into work by providing help with CVs, job applications and with more substantial barriers such as drug and alcohol problems. These contractors were paid on the basis of their record in moving claimants into work and keeping them there. Although it replaced Labour's Flexible New Deal, the Work Programme continued Labour's approach of giving contractors from the private and voluntary sectors the freedom to operate, guided only by the understanding that they would be paid solely on the basis of their results.

## iii. How effective has the single welfare-to-work programme been?

Despite some notable similarities, the cleanest break from Labour's welfare-to-work programmes came with the government's policy of rewarding contractors only once individuals participating on the programme had found and kept a job for at least six months (although this was reduced to three months for claimants with disabilities).

For most of its time in office Labour had measured the effectiveness of its programmes only upon how many participants had started a job. Its introduction in 2009 of the Flexible New Deal, however, began weighting the rewards towards how many people finding work were able to keep their job. But the bar was set at three months.

Contractors delivering the Work Programme were also given a two-year period to help all claimants find work, with payments made retrospectively once they had succeeded on this front, whereas the Flexible New Deal allotted one year per participant and offered contractors a lump sum up front with which they were expected to achieve their objectives.

What, then, have been the outcomes of the government's programme? 1.72 million people were referred to the Work Programme between June 2011 and March 2015. Of those, 432,610 (25%) achieved a 'job outcome' on the Work Programme – for most claimants this entailed finding and keeping a job for at least six months but, as we have said, the bar was lowered to three months for claimants with disabilities.

The Work Programme has been marginally more successful than its Labour predecessor, and at half the cost. It seems to have been more able to keep people in work for a longer period of time of at least six months. Table 1 gives an overall picture for each programme.

The Coalition's programme also broke new ground in opening its doors to Employment and Support

**Table 1:** Job outcomes of the Flexible New Deal, October 2009 to May 2011, and Work Programme, June 2011 to March 2015

|  | Number of claimants referred | Number of claimants who found jobs lasting up to six months | Number of claimants who found jobs lasting six months or more |
|---|---|---|---|
| **Flexible New Deal** | 407,690 | 75,250 (18.4%) | 49,740 (12.2%) |
| **Work Programme** | 1,720,000 | 28,130 (1.5%) | 404,480 (23.5%) |

Source: DWP statistical releases

Allowance claimants – generally comprising those who have been unable to work due to illness or disability – as well as those who were moved off Incapacity Benefit on the basis that they were fit for work. But the Work Programme's successes so far have been unevenly distributed amongst different claimant groups and between different parts of the country.

As we can see from Table 2, between June 2011 and March 2015, 34.1% of people aged under 25 and claiming Jobseeker's Allowance found a job through the Work Programme. According to the National Audit Office (NAO) they also had a far greater chance of keeping a job than had they taken part in Labour's welfare-to-work programmes.[1]

**Table 2:** Work Programme outcomes, June 2011 to March 2015

| Claimant Type | Number of claimants referred to the Work Programme | Number of claimants who found jobs | Proportion of claimants who found jobs |
|---|---|---|---|
| Aged 18-24, claiming JSA (entered after 9 months) | 298,710 | 101,870 | 34.1% |
| Aged over 25, claiming JSA (entered after 12 months) | 734,110 | 207,120 | 28.2% |
| Early Entrants, claiming JSA | 383,210 | 95,490 | 24.9% |
| New ESA claimants | 112,260 | 14,740 | 13.1% |
| Other ESA claimants | 199,440 | 13,390 | 6.7% |
| **TOTAL** | 1,727,730 | 432,610 | 25.0% |

Source: DWP statistical releases

Far less impressive is the record of people claiming Employment and Support Allowance being able to find and keep a job through the Work Programme. The government originally set a target for contractors of achieving a 'job outcome' for at least 22% of such claimants, although halfway through the last parliament it was forced to downgrade this expectation to 13%. Neither target had been met by the end of the parliament.

Likewise the Work Programme has performed relatively poorly for participants aged 50 and over. Of the 311,780 over-50s who were referred to the Work Programme between June 2011 and March 2015, 51,430 (16.5%) found and kept a job for at least three months. Data covering the period to December 2014 shows they were ten percentage points less likely to achieve a job outcome than participants aged between 25 and 49, and 18 percentage points less likely than those aged between 18 and 24.[2]

On these two fronts the government's record does not show any significant improvement on what went before. Although the previous Labour government did not oblige claimants with disabilities to join its main employment programmes, it did establish two separate voluntary initiatives: the New Deal for Disabled People which ran nationally between 2001 and 2006, and Pathways To Work from 2007 onwards.[3] Between 2001 and 2006, the New Deal for Disabled People accepted on a voluntary basis 260,330 people claiming incapacity benefits, of whom 110,950 (43%) found work. 59,080 of these jobs lasted at least three months.[4] The programme cost an estimated £204 million.[5]

How can we explain the New Deal for Disabled People's relatively healthy success rate? We need look no further than the government's own evaluation, which states:

> Participants were more likely to be male, younger, on benefits for a shorter period of time, less likely to have a mental health condition, but more likely to have musculoskeletal problems, more likely to state their health was fair, or [very] good and less

19

likely to say it was [very] bad, and more likely to have an educational qualification than the incapacity-related benefit population as a whole.[6]

The programme was therefore sailing with the tide and had, by its closure, largely succeeded in helping back into work those whose claims were short-term and who could be classed as closest to the labour market.

Labour's second employment programme for claimants with disabilities, Pathways To Work, sailed in choppier waters. It delivered a 'job outcome' rate of 15%, more akin to its successor, the Work Programme. Here lies the brick wall that Welfare Reform Mark Two will have to surmount. Claimants participating in Pathways To Work reported themselves as having

> mental health conditions, musculoskeletal and cardiovascular conditions, and... other conditions. However, it was common for people to describe... more than one kind of condition which affected their daily activities. Pain, fatigue and depression were common aspects of the lives of many people taking part, and medication to control symptoms often had further effect on memory or concentration, or caused people to sleep during parts of the day.[7]

The authors of the government's evaluation state later in the same report that, 'in retrospect, looking back over the year since initial contact with [Pathways To Work], the most important influence for many was their perception of their health'.[8]

Those tasked with evaluating the Work Programme identified similar difficulties facing claimants with disabilities who 'often described complex health conditions, and did not yet feel ready to make progress towards work. In these situations, they often indicated that there was little their adviser would be able to do about their health conditions in any case, perceiving this was the remit of their medical practitioner'.[9]

It would seem, therefore, that despite the more generous payments on offer to contractors to focus their efforts on claimants with disabilities, the tale between Labour's and Iain Duncan Smith's main employment programmes was one of continuity; job outcomes for this group of claimants will not exceed 15% unless the support offered is tailored to the health conditions that hinder claimants' abilities to perform some sort of work.

If the government is intent on opening up this second welfare reform front it need not look much further for a workable policy than its existing stock of programmes, for it launched in October 2010 an initiative called Work Choice which has enjoyed some success in helping people with disabilities into work, albeit on a limited scale. Claimants with long-term health conditions or illnesses join Work Choice voluntarily – the same basis on which they would have joined Labour's employment programmes for people with disabilities – and support is not limited to people claiming any particular benefit. Contractors are paid 70% of their fees upfront to deliver the programme so they are relatively well equipped to try and support claimants back into a position where they can find and keep work.

The official data suggests this strategy has reaped modest rewards. Of the 85,960 claimants who have taken part in Work Choice, 35,120 found work. 14,390 of this group were able to stay in work for at least six months.[10]

The government imposed a cap on the number of claimants who could take part in Work Choice. Its preferred route for most claimants was the Work

Programme. A cap was set also on the length of time claimants could take part in Work Choice without finding work.[11] We believe the lifting of both caps could help the government build on the programme's early success.

A separate voluntary employment programme may also boost the job prospects of claimants aged 50 and over. Following a trial run in October 1999, Labour in April 2000 rolled out a voluntary New Deal programme for the over-50s. Between 2003 and its closure in 2011, the period for which the government recorded data, almost all those enrolled (109,340 out of 115,840) on the New Deal 50+ started a job, and the programme cost around £80 million a year.[12] The data doesn't allow us to compare directly the New Deal 50+ with the Work Programme, as it doesn't show how many of the over-50s referred to each programme may have started work and left soon after. Yet while the outcomes of Labour's programme represent only a small number of additional jobs each year, and no data is held on the duration of these jobs, such a staggeringly high 'success rate' becomes that much more remarkable following our brief examination of the Work Programme's record.

How can these different 'success rates' for the Work Programme be explained and thereby understood? The old concerns around the mega private contractors creaming off the 'easier to help' claimants have yet to be answered. Despite the early fanfare from the Department for Work and Pensions, differential pricing has failed to have much impact so far on the likelihood of contractors taking an easy win by focusing their efforts on claimants requiring relatively little help to find work.

Contractors could earn themselves up to £13,120 for each Employment and Support Allowance claimant they place into work. This compares handsomely with the £3,410 on offer to find jobs for the young unemployed. Yet just 6.7% of longer-term Employment and Support Allowance claimants referred to the Work Programme have found and kept a job, despite the payments being weighted towards this group of claimants starting work. The department's own evaluation published in December 2014, found that 'payment groups have not significantly influenced the support being received by participants', and that only 'a minority of providers did try to target in respect of differential pricing'.[13] Most providers understandably dived for those claimants who they could most easily get into work. More worryingly, the report found less than 10% of Work Programme subcontractors made decisions based on payment fees. Between the 18 prime contractors paid to deliver the Work Programme, there are 858 subcontractors.

Differential pricing was just one of the means through which the Work Programme was designed to improve upon Labour's employment programmes. But what of its overall effectiveness? While evidence from Iain Duncan Smith's first five years suggests that both he and Labour met some measure of success, the Work Programme so far has delivered only patchy improvements on what had gone before, but at half the cost, and well over 60% of unemployed claimants taking part in welfare-to-work programmes have been left 'parked' on benefit under both governments.

Most telling in this respect is the Work Programme's performance among Jobseeker's Allowance claimants aged 25 and over – the largest cohort to participate in the programme. Contractors expected at the outset to find work for 42% of claimants in this group, while the department set a lower bar of 39%. Its bare minimum expectation was 33%. Yet for those claimants who completed two years on the programme it failed to live up to any of these expectations, delivering a success rate of 27% and, with it, only a one percentage point improvement on Labour's Flexible New Deal.

While the long-term unemployed who joined the Work Programme more recently seem to have fared better, time will tell whether this has been due to improvements in the programme itself or more generally in the availability of jobs in the economy. The National Audit Office predicts that 38% of those participants whose placement continued beyond April 2014 had found and kept a job for at least six months, compared with 34% whose Flexible New Deal placement lasted the same length of time.[14]

The most notable breakthrough that came with the Work Programme has been to help successful jobseekers remain in work for longer. Yet if the Work Programme is to become an all-out success the government will need to reform it in such a way that it is able to deliver much improved outcomes for people with disabilities and those aged over 50, while ensuring those getting and keeping a job are able subsequently to increase their earnings. We return to these themes in our postscript.

## iv. How do the costs compare with previous programmes?

The cost of Labour's Flexible New Deal came in at £770 million over two years to October 2011. Just over £1 billion had been spent on the Work Programme in its first two years to September 2013, and the government estimated the total cost to the taxpayer of the Work Programme would be between £3 billion and £5 billion over the six years to 2017. Looking only at the cost of both programmes per Jobseeker's Allowance claimant, the National Audit Office puts them neck and neck at £1,500 apiece.[15] Yet overall the Centre for Economic and Social Inclusion and the National Institute of Adult Continuing Education, in evidence submitted to the Work and Pensions Committee at the beginning of the 2015 parliament, estimated that the Work Programme had achieved 'outcomes that are comparable with the programmes that it replaced... at a much lower unit cost (perhaps around half the cost, on a per participant basis, than the programmes it replaced)'.[16]

Again we are presented with a picture of incremental improvement, rather than one of revolutionary change under Iain Duncan Smith, whereby a steady stream of claimants enrolled on welfare-to-work programmes are indeed helped into work, but many others remain dependent on out-of-work benefit.

## v. Youth unemployment

The 2010 Conservative manifesto specifically mentioned the plight of the young unemployed under Labour, suggesting that 'we are at risk of creating a lost generation of young people without the skills to participate in the workforce, without hope for the future'.[17] The two main programmes initiated by the previous Labour government in an attempt to tackle youth unemployment were the New Deal for Young People and the Future Jobs Fund.

The New Deal for Young People was introduced in 1998. Receipt of Jobseeker's Allowance for young people aged 24 and under was made conditional after six months on taking part in the New Deal for Young People (which is not to be confused with Franklin D. Roosevelt's job creation scheme of the 1930s). At the six month stage of their claim the young unemployed were given additional support to apply for jobs, combined with the offer of training or work experience. Between 1998 and 2005, 1,292,890 young people joined the New Deal for Young People, of whom 446,490 (34.5%) found and kept hold of a job for at least three months. Total expenditure over these seven years came to £2.71 billion.

Although it was judged at the time to have been broadly successful, the National Audit Office cautioned that the New Deal for Young People did not necessarily create new jobs for claimants. Its success was in being able to place young people into a labour market which, at the time, was creating jobs aplenty.[18] Concerns were raised, too, around the worryingly large number of familiar faces who remained out of work and were being recycled through the programme. Even if they found work, for one reason or another participants struggled to keep a job for more than three months and were destined all too often to be back on benefit.

The programme could be classed, therefore, as a qualified success. It met the Labour government's objectives of placing 250,000 young people into work, but was aided in its quest by an extraordinarily benign economic environment. The programme was found wanting when it came to keeping young people in work for a sustained period of time.

Labour had inherited a youth unemployment rate of 14.3% (656,000 young unemployed workers), and at the end of its first term this reached a trough of 11.7% (527,000 young unemployed workers). Yet after a decade of Labour in power and continuous economic growth the rate had climbed to 14.7% and the number to 711,000.

Arguably Labour's most successful welfare-to-work initiative, and the programme which broke new ground, came in 2009 when the government was tasked with trying to handle the economic crisis. The then chancellor of the exchequer, Alistair Darling, set aside £1 billion for a new programme, the Future Jobs Fund, which offered subsidies to employers to create paid jobs for young people at risk of becoming long-term unemployed.[19] Those on the scheme received at least the National Minimum Wage for their work, and were given basic help in how to present themselves to a future employer, looking for more permanent jobs and a supplement toward travel costs.

Its impact on youth unemployment was immediate. The Future Jobs Fund created its first job in September 2009, following a year in which 160,000 more young people found themselves on the dole and the youth unemployment rate had increased by 4.2 percentage points. The Future Jobs Fund within its first three months had cut the rate by 0.5 percentage points and the number by 33,000.[20]

Why, then, was it scrapped by the Coalition government? The Future Jobs Fund was a notable victim of the cuts programme set out by David Laws, the then Liberal Democrat chief secretary to the Treasury, within a month of the Coalition's advent. He sought to justify the programme's closure by claiming it was not providing value for money. Clearly it was too early to draw such conclusions. Long after the government moved to close the scheme, it was found that the Future Jobs Fund had created jobs for more than 100,000 young people during the deepest troughs of the recession, and delivered net benefits of £7,750 per participant to society.[21]

How does the Future Jobs Fund compare to the Youth Contract, a similar initiative launched specifically in April 2012 by the then deputy prime minister, Nick Clegg, to counter youth unemployment? Although no mention was made of setting up the Youth Contract in 'The Coalition: our programme for government', this was a specific response from the government to high and rising levels of youth unemployment during its first two years in office. The government set the Youth Contract the objective of helping low-skilled NEETs (young people defined as 'Not in Education, Employment or Training'), care-leavers and young offenders into work or training. Despite the Department for Work and Pensions initially estimating that there were 70,000 such individuals who would be helped into work by providing employers with a wage incentive of £2,275 – barely more than a third of the subsidy offered under the Future Jobs Fund – it later revised this forecast to less than half of the total client group of 70,000 starting a paid work placement before the scheme would end in March 2016.[22] By November 2014, two and a half years into the scheme, just 16,540 young people participating in the Youth Contract had completed a work placement of six months. £1 billion was set aside by the Coalition to see through the Youth Contract, but by the end of 2013-14 its true cost had come to £296 million.

The Youth Contract could best be described as a watered down version of the Future Jobs Fund, in respect of its funding, provision and outcomes. In just a year and a half covering the deepest recession the country has ever experienced the Future Jobs Fund created jobs for 100,000 young people. Its successor, the Youth Contract, is on course to create a third of these jobs over a four-year period spanning a rapid economic recovery.

The overall level of youth unemployment under the government has fluctuated with the fortunes of the wider economy, as well as the general performance of the Work Programme for young Jobseeker's Allowance claimants. It inherited 939,000 young unemployed, and a rate of 20.1%.

Youth unemployment peaked at the halfway stage of the 2010 parliament, at 1.05 million and 22.5% respectively. Thanks largely to the upturn in the economy and the improved performance of the Work Programme the government went into the 2015 election having cut youth unemployment to 738,000 and a rate of 16%.

# vi. Conclusion

We have shown here how the welfare-to-work tools with which the government has sought to prod people into work have achieved mixed results. The government has been:

- Slightly more successful than Labour in getting the long-term unemployed into work

- Seemingly[23] much more successful than Labour in keeping them in work for a longer period of time, and at half the cost

- Not very successful in finding work for claimants with disabilities and those aged over 50

- Wrong to scrap Labour's Future Jobs Fund before evidence had emerged of its success or failure, but the Work Programme was relatively successful in placing young people into the jobs aplenty being created during the economic recovery spanning the second half of the parliament.

What of the other means through which work was to be incentivised? We pick up on this theme in the following section on the conditions attached to drawing benefit.

# 3

## Swinging the pendulum of conditionality: making work the easier option

### i. Phases of conditionality

There have been five phases in which the debate on conditionality shifted in the post-war period. Clement Attlee would have thought that the sun would cease to rise if strict rules of conditionality had not applied to the drawing of benefit. Because most social security in the immediate post-war period was National Insurance-based, and the ability to continue drawing benefit was based strictly on the payment of contributions in what were called the relevant contributory years, Attlee's moral order needed little safeguarding.

Beatrice Webb, a midwife to Fabianism, the Labour Party, its early policy, and much else besides, thought that given the current state of human nature, awarding benefits unconditionally was simply 'madness'.[1] William Beveridge was clear that the receipt of benefit had to be conditional, both in respect of contributions and of conduct while claiming benefit. Yet Beveridge's conditionality was later to be undermined.

A second front opened up in the conditionality debate in the 1960s when the argument was launched that welfare should be made far less conditional. This was at a time when welfare's National Insurance base was being undermined by the failure to maintain the real value of contributory benefits against average earnings, and politicians were opting increasingly for the distribution of welfare based on the means-test. The great intellectual driving force in arguing for a less and less conditionally-based welfare state was Richard Titmuss, whose influence on the welfare debate in this country is still to be fully judged. Titmuss's belief was that the West was about to enter into an age of economic abundance. The task in the future would not be one of how to limit benefits, but how to increase the scope and the take-up of such benefits in an age of unknown abundance.[2]

That age of abundance did not arrive. Indeed the opposite occurred only too soon with the beginnings in the 1970s of the oil crisis which led to a quadrupling of oil prices in the space of a single year and a marked downturn in the world economy. Only three decades later did the global economy appear to recover.[3] Yet the age of scarcity remained in the political subconscious with too many politicians being bitten with the idea of unconditional welfare.

The political beginnings of a backlash to the Titmuss line began very tentatively under Margaret Thatcher when the most elementary requirements in drawing Unemployment Benefit were reintroduced. She had initially broken the link between signing on for work and the payment of benefits under some bizarre advice from Sir Derek Rayner, who advised Mrs Thatcher on improving government efficiency, for saving public expenditure!

A first step back towards conditionality was taken in July 1986 when the then employment secretary, Lord Young, rolled out the Restart initiative. This programme entailed job centre staff asking all those who had been unemployed for a year or more to enrol on an activity designed to help them back into work. It was compulsory for claimants to undertake this activity if they wished to continue drawing benefit and avoid having a sanction imposed upon their claim.

Tony Blair's government continued this gentle tip-toeing onto a new position on conditionality. Labour left untouched for a decade the circumstances job centre staff should take into account when deciding whether or not to apply a sanction, the level and duration of sanctions, procedures for challenging sanction decisions, and hardship provision for claimants subject to sanctions. It did, however, widen the net of conditionality so that the obligations to prepare for work were applied to new claimant groups, such as lone parents and the sick or disabled. This increased the number of claimants to whom benefit sanctions could be applied.

The following period we refer to as one of hesitant conditionality – both Labour and the Tories remained surprisingly reluctant to grasp the nettle for which they would have had so much public support and which was crucial if public opinion was to maintain its confidence in the welfare system. Throughout this period, from 2008 until the birth of the Coalition government in 2010, incremental steps were taken to deepen the obligations on lone parents to undertake at least some activity to prepare themselves for work. From April 2008 lone parents with children aged 12 and under were required twice a year to attend a 'work-focused interview' with Jobcentre Plus, and from November of the same year all lone parents whose youngest child was aged over 12 were moved from Income Support to Jobseeker's Allowance.

A fifth era in the march back to conditionality was clearly marked in the 'Jobs and Welfare' section of the Coalition's programme for government: 'We will ensure that receipt of benefits for those able to work is conditional on their willingness to work.' This was a phrase that politicians had used before in their attempt to quell voter unrest at what was perceived to be the ease of drawing benefit, and for which the working population was called upon to pay. But the government moved beyond words and into action. So began the one reform that will have a more long-term and lasting impact on welfare as we have known it than all the other reforms the government has introduced. In 19 words the government gave notice that welfare for working-age claimants would cease to be unconditional, bringing down the final curtain on the ideology of unconditional welfare that had so mysteriously captured the thinking of politicians in the early 1960s.[4] Action followed.

How has the intent of abolishing welfare as we have known it fared in practice? As so often in respect of major structural reforms, and even more so in culturally driven ones, the pendulum is pushed so far in the opposite direction that different and equally disturbing injustices occur in place of the ones with which the reform set out to deal. Hence the need for constant vigilance on how a major reform is working out in practice. A willingness to modify is not a sign of weakness but of exercising real statecraft. In our judgment such statecraft was lacking in respect of the government's sanctions policy which became the central agent of this new approach to conditionality.

The claimant contract setting out one's duties while drawing benefit was first introduced in 1996 as the Jobseeker's Agreement and then appeared in its current form, the Claimant Commitment, in 2013. We welcome the idea of a claimant contract for it necessarily develops the idea of a contract-based society where citizens are aware of what their duties are and how those duties need to be performed before rights are earned. Our concern with the current Claimant Commitment is that the duties, while clearly spelled out, are not buttressed by a counterbalancing series of safeguards or rights. Indeed, the words 'safeguards' and 'rights' are missing completely from the contract. We nevertheless accept that, in moving to a contract-based society, a first step has to be taken, and we welcome the Claimant Commitment as that first step. But we do believe, based on what evidence the Department for Work and Pensions has published, that it is now in urgent need of rebalancing. The contract is so dominated by phrases such as 'you must' that it reads as though it has fallen from a prison manual. It is on this basis of a 'you must' culture, unbuttressed by 'we will', that the sanctions policy has been built.

Until October 2012 sanctions could be applied to Jobseeker's Allowance claimants if they failed to meet one of the key conditions outlined in the claimant contract without 'good cause'. Sanctions were for fixed periods or of a variable length.

Fixed length sanctions of one, two, four or 26 weeks were imposed for a failure without good cause to attend or participate in an interview or welfare-to-work programme, or carry out a specific instruction from a

Jobcentre Plus adviser. Importantly, payment of benefit continued in full pending a decision on the imposition of a sanction. Although the government's conditionality reforms leave this regulation in place, a further longstanding regulation allows Jobcentre Plus to 'suspend' a claim if doubts arise as to whether a claimant has undertaken the necessary activities to prepare themselves for work. If suspicion on this front leads Jobcentre Plus to suspend a claim, payment of benefit ceases immediately. The government does not publish data on the number of claimants whose money has been docked in this way.

Varied length sanctions of between one and 26 weeks were imposed under the previous regime for failures to comply with basic requirements, such as refusing employment without good cause, or losing employment through misconduct. The actual period of suspension in each case was at the discretion of the 'decision maker' – a member of staff who decides on benefit claims and does not deal face to face with claimants.

Three main changes were introduced in 2012 by the government:

- three categories of sanction became operative and depended on the nature of the 'offence';

- different fixed durations of sanction now exist for first, second and third offences;

- the new sanction period now begins on the first day of the week in which the offence occurred, or the first day of the week following the date the claimant last received Jobseeker's Allowance.

The 'independence' of the decision-making continues in the new regime, although the fairness of the system as it works out in practice is open for debate.

Lower level sanctions are applied to claimants who, for example, fail to attend an interview with their Jobcentre Plus adviser. These sanctions lead to claimants losing all of their Jobseeker's Allowance for a fixed period of four weeks for the first failure and any further failures within the next two weeks, followed by 13 weeks for subsequent failures within the next year.

Intermediate level sanctions are applied to those who, for example, make themselves unavailable for work. They apply likewise for four weeks following a first failure and any repeat failure within two weeks, rising to 13 weeks for subsequent failures in the following year.

Higher level sanctions are applied for those leaving a job voluntarily or failing to take up the offer of work experience, for example. Claimants lose all of their Jobseeker's Allowance for a fixed period of 13 weeks for a first offence and any further offence committed within the following two weeks, 26 weeks for a second offence within the next year and 156 weeks for a third and subsequent offence.

This dramatic change in the role conditionality now plays in welfare has clearly put strains on Department for Work and Pensions staff in carrying out their duties in an effective but humane way. The numbers of staff have been progressively reduced and, although the claimant count is down, the scope for officers deciding upon the sanctions has been very significantly increased.

The sanctions policy as initiated by Iain Duncan Smith appears from the reports published by voluntary organisations, to whom some might refer as the Big Society, to be causing havoc and despair amongst a growing number of claimants.[5] Judgment is at the essence here. Clearly a tougher sanctions regime is required to be applied against those who have grown accustomed to swinging the lead at taxpayers' expense. But for others, sometimes confused, often frightened, and for others who have difficulty understanding formal procedures, and others still just simply worn down by the circumstances of their lot, these sanctions sentences cut incomes to a far higher degree than any magistrates court is empowered to do, and then can only do after exercising its independent judgment based on the 'facts' presented in open court.

Worse still, the sanctions policy has moved so fast in the direction against claimants that many of them are unsure of what the 'charge' is they are expected to refute, let alone know how to dispute that 'charge'.[6] We believe the sanctions regime as it stands has become too rigid, too complex, too harsh, and is applied under conditions that appear to be unfavourable to claimants. All too many claimants appear to be subjected to a disproportionately arbitrary punishment for a simple and genuine mistake, or a piece of sheer misfortune such as their bus arriving late to take them to their Jobcentre Plus appointment.[7]

The data show that between 2010 and 2015, 3.54 million sanction decisions led to a claimant losing their Jobseeker's Allowance for a set period. Detailed statistics are published only for the period between October 2012 and March 2015, during which 1.81 million sanctions were applied.[8] There is therefore no possibility of comparing the sanctions policy with that operating up to 2012, let alone 2010. The headline figure for this 2012-15 period is clear; benefit was withdrawn from 971,348 Jobseeker's Allowance claimants.[9] Many of these claimants suffered a series of sanctions being applied against them:

- One sanction was applied in 861,055 cases.

- Two sanctions were applied in 188,119 cases.

- Three or more sanctions were applied in 121,089 cases.

Yet this data throws up a slight mismatch between the numbers sanctioned (971,348), the numbers the government claims were sanctioned on one, two, three or more occasions (1.17 million) and the number of sanctions applied (1.81 million). We would welcome clarification from the Department for Work and Pensions on how many claimants are sanctioned once, twice, three times or more.

A similar mismatch arises in the data released separately by the Department for Work and Pensions, which tells us:[10]

- Decisions to apply a low- or intermediate-level sanction – which entails a loss of benefit for either four or 13 weeks – were made on 1,026,769 occasions.

- Decisions to apply a high-level sanction – which entails loss of benefit for either 13 weeks, six months or three years – were made on 137,627 occasions.

We are at a loss to state with any certainty how many claimants actually lost their benefit for certain periods of time as some claimants could, of course, have been sanctioned once, twice, or three times. Again we would welcome clarification on this score.

Although the department does not collect data on the impact of its sanctions policy, it is clear from information and research that has been published that a number of claimants – we know not how large a number – are being pushed permanently outside the benefits system, leading to some being totally disconnected from both work and welfare. This group is left to the protection of their parents, often elderly, and often poor themselves, or to the charity of friends, should such friends exist, and should they be able to help. Such a state of affairs has not been seen since the abolition of the Poor Law in 1948. Before the 2015 general election the government admitted in evidence to the then Work and Pensions Committee that it did not know where a third of people ended up after they had been sanctioned.[11] The number of sanctions was halved in the year leading up to the 2015 election, but it still remained at 506,502. Sanctions are therefore being applied at a scale unknown since the Second World War, and the operation of sanctions on this scale makes for the most significant change in the social security system as it has existed in the post-war period. Our main recommendation to the government is that it forthwith initiates a follow-up survey to see what happens to those claimants losing benefit.

In an independent review of the previous Labour government's conditionality policy, Paul Gregg argued that the use of sanctions is effective in changing behaviour as long as the employment programmes onto which people are placed are effective.[12] He believed sanctions had to be present within the system, to underpin the obligations and take on the role of a backstop for those failing to fulfil their duties. But he also emphasised how this must be a last resort. He therefore concluded that risks to claimants from a conditionality policy must be buttressed by a proper sense of fair play and safeguards implemented when sanctions are applied to particularly vulnerable groups.

An indicator that the current sanctions policy may not be working properly is the number of people, hungry, who resort to food banks after being sanctioned. We estimate that in 2014 between a sixth and a quarter of food bank referrals took place following a sanction.[13] Of course, some of those sanctioned will have broken the rules and may have refused job offers or failed to turn up for interviews. However, given the impact of just a four-week sanction on an individual and their family, let alone one for a whole year or more, the decision to place sanctions should not be taken without fair and clearly understood warnings, with sanctions only following the claimant's failure to complete the responsibilities they clearly understand as part of their contract.

We therefore welcome Iain Duncan Smith's decision to pilot a 'Yellow Card' warning system – as recommended by the All-Party Parliamentary Inquiry into Hunger in the United Kingdom – whereby claimants are given a warning of the government's intention to apply a sanction, and a 14-day period to provide a justifiable reason for failing to meet the terms of their Claimant Commitment, before the decision to sanction is made. The Department for Work and Pensions will then review this information before deciding whether a sanction remains appropriate. We very much welcome this development and we expect the department to publish the results of this trial early in 2017.

We believe it is those claimants who should be able to prove with ease that they have a justifiable reason for missing an appointment at Jobcentre Plus, for example, who are most likely to be protected by the introduction of a Yellow Card warning system.

Should the Yellow Card fail to prevent injustices from occurring, the government might wish to supplement this policy with the option for Jobcentre Plus staff of issuing a non-financial sanction for a claimant's first failure to meet the terms of their Claimant Commitment.

A most worrying sign remains the government's lack of knowledge on a claimant's next move after they've been sanctioned. The best estimates suggest around 20% of those leaving benefit following a sanction report finding work; but the fate of the remaining 80% is anybody's guess.[14] As is the total amount of benefit expenditure withdrawn through the application of sanctions. How are we to judge the effectiveness or otherwise of a policy if its impact on poverty, employment and public expenditure remains a mystery? Moreover, as the CSJ notes:

> The performance measure that [Jobcentre Plus] uses, the so-called 'off-flow rate' which measures the number of people who cease to receive their particular benefit, is misleading and can be counter-productive ... this current measure does not provide a complete picture of the performance of [Jobcentre Plus]... [15]

The government's policy in respect of the welfare roll was made clear in its 2011 Performance Management Framework, 'with the clear and shared objective of moving customers off benefits as rapidly as possible'.[16] The authors behind the official evaluation of this policy stated that, 'one possible negative externality that could be related to the [Performance Measurement Framework] flows from not currently having the "into employment" element in the data at the time of the fieldwork'.[17] The authors were also concerned that 'one way of producing off-flows from benefit is through sanctioning jobseekers'.[18]

What then of people not claiming benefit but also not in work?[19] Worryingly, the number of people ceasing to claim Jobseeker's Allowance whose destination is unknown almost doubled under Labour, from 1.02 million (32% of claimants leaving Jobseeker's Allowance) in 1998 to 1.96 million (50%) in 2010. While the overall number since then has fallen to 1.51 million, the proportion has increased again to 52%.[20]

## ii. Conclusion

We believe it must be one's duty while drawing Jobseeker's Allowance to look for work: conditionality is part of a contract which entails benefit payments being dependent on satisfying this duty. But this principle has now been so applied to an ever greater number of working-age recipients, and in what appears to be an industrial scale operation to remove them from the welfare rolls, that mass injustices could be occurring and genuine claimants risk being exposed to destitution.

Widespread concern has been expressed on the justice inherent in the mass application of sanctions. The government announced in February 2015 that it was about to begin trialling the threat of sanctions against people in low-paid work, should they fail to increase their earnings through more hours or a higher hourly wage. By the time of the 2015 election the names of these pilots had not been disclosed.

We comment in the postscript on the next stage in erecting a sanctions system that is both effective and knows the impact on individuals who have been properly warned about the potential consequences of not fulfilling their Claimant Commitment. And we repeat our major recommendation that the government commissions an independent body to trace a sample of claimants sanctioned, to report on their wellbeing, and for this report to be published.

It is beyond doubt, for now, that the government's conditionality policy makes life in work that much more preferable to being on benefit, but this policy has come with a social cost – the size of which remains unknown – of people being pushed outside the worlds of both work and welfare.

We turn our attention now to the impact of the government's reforms to Working and Child Tax Credits, Housing Benefit and Council Tax Benefit on its overall objective of making work the best route out of poverty.

# 4

# Raising the bar to making work pay

## i. Cutting the subsidy to low pay

The British economy has long been characterised by the issue of low pay. Back in 1971 the then Conservative government reverted to a Speenhamland system of subsidising low wages, so that workers' pay could be brought up to a more acceptable minimum.[1] Since then wage subsidies have grown like no other part of the welfare state:

- In 1971 the Family Income Supplement was introduced which soon had 71,000 claims being met, at a cost in today's money of £42 million.

- 17 years later in 1988 another Conservative government changed Family Income Supplement into what was then called Family Credit. 261,000 low-paid workers in that year claimed this supplement to their pay at a cost of £826 million in today's money.

- This Family Credit total increased again to 1.2 million claimants in 1999 before Labour introduced what was called the Working Families' Tax Credit. The value of the subsidy paid out in that year had already reached £3.4 billion in today's money.

- In 2003, the final year of Working Families' Tax Credit, 1.4 million low-paid workers in Britain claimed the subsidy at a cost in today's money of £8.5 billion.

- Its successors, Working and Child Tax Credits, were being claimed by 4.9 million low-paid workers across the UK in 2011, the peak year of payments. The bill that taxpayers met for this subsidy in that year came to £30.5 billion in today's money.

The government since 2010 has sought to grapple with this growing taxpayer subsidy to low wages, not by a policy of attempting to increase real wages, and therefore making families less eligible for the wage supplement, but only by restricting eligibility to tax credits.

The severity of the means-test, by which a percentage of benefits are withdrawn as income rises, was increased barely a month following the Coalition government's advent in 2010. This percentage, or what feels to claimants like a marginal tax rate, was raised from 39% to 41%. This is estimated to have saved the government around £700 million a year. A more aggressive withdrawal of benefit from households in which both people work came in the reduction from 2012 of the second income threshold; by an extraordinary amount, from £40,000 to £15,860. In practice this meant that whereas the marginal tax rate of 41% previously would have applied only to families earning at least £40,000, from 2012 it was extended to all those earning £15,860 and above. Yet this move against two-wage earner households saved the government only a modest estimated £130 million a year.

The removal of the Baby Element of tax credits, a supplement that could be claimed by families with a child aged under one, saved around £275 million a year, and the reduction in the backdating period for new claims and changes of circumstances, from three months to one, saved around £350 million a year. Alongside this the percentage of childcare costs payable from tax credits was reduced from 80% to 70% from April 2011, saving £270 million in 2011-12 and around £690 million in each subsequent year.

A second front in the Coalition's attempt to cut or at least contain tax credit costs opened in April 2012:

- Couples with children were required to work a combined total of at least 24 hours per week to become eligible for tax credits, up from 16 hours per week. This move alone cut the tax credit bill by around £500 million a year.

- The basic rate paid to all claimants, and the additional rate of up to £810 each year paid to claimants working 30 hours a week, were frozen in cash terms for three years (saving £270 million in the first year and rising to £750 million in 2013-14, and £975 million in 2014-15).

- The 50-plus return-to-work bonus was abolished, saving around £30 million a year.

The effect on household incomes of the 2012 reforms was far from modest. The Institute for Fiscal Studies estimates that lone parents earning £15,600 were made up to £868 a year worse off.[2] The eligibility restrictions resulted in 1.6 million fewer claims from working households being made by April 2014, and the total wage subsidy fell in real terms by £1.6 billion from its peak in 2011 to April 2015.[3]

Behind the opening of this reform front was the recognition that tax credits have played a part in subsidising the creation of part-time jobs offering short hours at the National Minimum Wage. Earnings accrued from such jobs alone could never guarantee a life free from poverty. Hence the dependency of so many workers, and the employers offering these jobs, on tax credits. Having set out to curtail the cost of this subsidy to low-paying employers, the government is looking now to Universal Credit to set a minimum working week of 35 hours at the National Living Wage for those aged 25 and over. Such a commitment to help increase the living standards of people entering work is laudable. However, as we outline later in this audit, a number of obstacles to this commitment have been erected elsewhere within the government's plans for Universal Credit. Their net effect will be to make this commitment almost impossible to fulfil. Reformers looking to maximise household incomes by encouraging people into work, and helping them advance once there, will face an uphill struggle under the government's current plans.

Reformers were left contemplating a further series of obstacles being strewn across their uphill climb towards the summit of fixing 'broken Britain', following the opening of a third tax credit reform front in the 2015 Summer Budget, under which:

- Child Tax Credit would be limited to two children for new claimants from April 2017.

- The amount by which a claimant's income can increase before their award changes would be reduced from £5,000 to £2,500 in April 2016.

- The Family Element would no longer be awarded from April 2017 when a first child is born.

- The rate at which tax credits are clawed back from claimants would increase from 41% to 48% from April 2016.

- The level of earnings at which tax credits begin to be clawed back would be lowered from £6,420 to £3,850 from April 2016.

It became all too clear following the Summer Budget that the latter two measures alone would cut £4.35 billion from the tax credit bill in April 2016. In combination they would have formed the biggest single cut ever imposed on tax credit claimants, with 3.2 million working households losing an average of £1,350. Their effect would have been to levy on low-paid workers an effective tax increase of seven pence in the pound.

Hence the collective sigh of relief heaved by this group of grafters when the chancellor announced in his 2015 Autumn Statement, following an almighty cross-party campaign in both Houses of Parliament, that he was abandoning these two measures.

Taking into consideration the overall package of tax credit reforms enacted since 2010, it should come as no surprise that the government has not only prevented the tax credit bill growing at what had been the underlying growth rate, but it has actually made some inroads into the total bill. The cost has been borne, though, both by new and existing claimants and, because the system does not allow one to remove eligibility from higher earners without impacting on all claimants, those with higher incomes as well as many others in low-paid work have shared the losses.

A further cut of £4.35 billion would have been one cut too far to the living standards of low-paid workers – that very group of voters the chancellor was so keen to court before, during and since the last general election.

## ii. Cutting the subsidy to high rents

Coupled with the low wages paid by many of the new jobs created since 2010, a topic to which we return in the following chapter, there has been a startling reversal in fortunes in Britain's housing market which has helped push up the Housing Benefit bill both before and since the government took office.

Under the previous Labour government real terms expenditure on Housing Benefit grew from £16.9 billion in 1996-97 to £22.2 billion in 2009-10. Despite introducing a raft of measures to try to contain this expenditure, it has continued to grow since 2010, by 10.4% in real terms, up to £24.5 billion in 2014-15.

What are the drivers behind this £8.6 billion increase, under successive governments, in the landlord subsidy? According to the House of Commons Library we can attribute 42% of the increase in Housing Benefit expenditure over the past two decades to the growing number of people paying soaring rents in the private sector. 1.62 million private tenants were drawing Housing Benefit in the year leading up to the 2015 election – 588,000 more than when Labour came to power in 1997, and 300,000 more than when Labour left office in 2010. Private tenants' average weekly claim increased in real terms between 1997 and 2015 from £92.76 to £108.10, although it had peaked in Labour's last year in office at £121.44, which gives some indication of the success of the government's assault on the costs of Housing Benefit. The Office for Budget Responsibility found in its analysis of Housing Benefit expenditure that in 2012-13 the number of private renters exceeded the number of social renters for the first time in almost 50 years (i.e. since the post-war boom in public housebuilding), and, as private rents are on average higher than social rents, this shift was a prime culprit for the upward pressure on Housing Benefit expenditure.[4]

Under the Library's calculations, the remaining 58% of the upward pressure on expenditure is accounted for by developments in the social rented sector. Here the reduction in the number of claimants – from 3.55 million in 1997 to 3.31 million in 2015 – relieved around 13% of the pressure on the Housing Benefit budget, but this was more than offset by the higher real-terms rents charged by housing associations to tenants remaining in the social rented sector. The average weekly claim from social housing tenants increased in real terms most under Labour from £60.63 to £81.45, but then again since 2010 to £87.96.

The net effect of the past decade's rent increases on tenants, renting privately or with a housing association, was to increase the proportion of household income required to cover net rent from 12.9% in 2002-3 (the first year for which consistent data is available) to 17.1% in 2010, and again to 18.9% in 2013.[5] Hence the growing need for support from taxpayers to minimise the chances of being served with an eviction order.

Politicians of all stripes agree that a main cause of higher prices and rents is the shortage of homes – either for owner-occupation, in social ownership, or for private renting. In contrast with Harold Macmillan's pledge to build over 300,000 homes a year, recent governments have failed to build anything like the number of homes Britain needs to keep up with changes in the population.

During the post-war period the number of new dwellings peaked in 1968 at 352,000, of which 149,220 were new social dwellings. In 2010 just 106,720 new dwellings were built – the lowest number of new homes built in any year since 1946 – of which a mere 23,440 were new social dwellings. Since then the overall number of new homes increased slightly in 2011 to 113,350, and again in 2012 to 115,340, before declining once more in 2013 to 109,640.

The net effect of these trends in housebuilding has been to increase the difficulties for ordinary working families to buy a home:

- The average price paid by first-time buyers increased, in real terms, from £198,000 in 2009, Labour's final year in office, to £202,000 in 2014.

- The ratio of house prices to earnings for first-time buyers rose from 4.4 when Labour left office in 2010 to 5.1 at the time of the 2015 election.

- The average age of first-time buyers rose by one year under the Coalition, from 29 to 30.

Not surprisingly given these longer-term trends, a look at the number of renters claiming Housing Benefit shows an important change in the composition of groups claiming benefit. Pensioners as a group are becoming less and less dependent on drawing Housing Benefit – a sign of success in tackling pensioner poverty. The overall numbers claiming Housing Benefit fell by 257,000 under Labour in the decade prior to the recession. But this fall was accounted for entirely by pensioners, as the number of working-age claimants remained static.

Moreover the forecast growth of 1.31 million in the numbers of working-age claimants (from 2.62 million to 3.93 million) over the decade to 2018-19 will more than offset the continuing decline by 0.3 million in the number of pensioner claimants (from 1.54 million to 1.24 million). The total number of claimants is therefore forecast to rise by just over 1 million in a decade.

As of 2015, more than halfway through this forecast period, there are 3.5 million households of working-age relying on Housing Benefit, out of a total caseload of 5 million households. By the end of the decade these successive figures are forecast by the Department for Work and Pensions to reach 3.9 million and 5.1 million respectively.

A significant source of upward pressure on the working-age Housing Benefit caseload and expenditure since 2010 has been the growing number of people in work whose wages are not high enough to cover rent. The proportion of Housing Benefit claims made by people in work increased by more than nine percentage points, from 13.7% (650,551) in May 2010 to 22.8% (1,103,100) in May 2015. The Office for Budget Responsibility puts this down to the weakness of average wage growth relative to rent inflation.[6]

How then has the government attempted to rein in expenditure on Housing Benefit for working-age claimants while subsequently incentivising work? We examine here its three chosen measures: the Benefit Cap, Local Housing Allowance reforms, and the Bedroom Tax.

## The Benefit Cap

Despite there being no mention nor any hint of such a proposal in 'The Coalition: our programme for government', since April 2013 a household benefit cap has applied to households claiming Housing Benefit or Universal Credit. Its prime objective is to ensure no family out of work can receive a higher income than the average family in work. Of all the reforms introduced by the government, this is the one which has had the most immediate effect on work incentives.

The cap applies either to Universal Credit or total income from Housing Benefit, Income Support, Jobseeker's Allowance, and Employment and Support Allowance. Households in receipt of Working Tax Credit, Personal Independence Payment or Disability Living Allowance are exempt from the cap. The cap was set in 2013 at £350 a week for childless single claimants, and £500 a week for lone parents or members of couples – the latter being equivalent to gross annual earnings of £35,000, and £26,000 net. It has largely affected families with large numbers of children and/or high rental costs.

Of the 58,700 households subject to the cap between April 2013 and February 2015, 14,400 (24.5%) responded by finding work and, as a result, gained exemption from the cap.[7] That's almost the same success rate as the Work Programme. Moving even into part-time work can have a most dramatic impact on family income. A single parent with five children in Wirral had the cap applied to her. When she was helped to find a job by the Troubled Families programme,[8] her income increased substantially back to its previous level. More importantly she reported her two eldest children saying how proud they were of her for having a job and made much of her achievement amongst their peers. Although it currently produces headline savings of 'only' £185 million a year – a mere 0.09% total welfare spending – its symbolic importance is very significant.

Two further measures were introduced to control expenditure; one affecting private tenants and the other social tenants.

## Local Housing Allowance

The government introduced in April 2011 a series of reforms to the Housing Benefit supplement, known as Local Housing Allowance, paid to private tenants living in areas where rents are particularly high:

- The Local Housing Allowance was capped in April 2011 at the 30th percentile of local private sector rents, as opposed to the 50th (median) percentile.

- The entitlement to up to £15 per week over and above rent that claimants were entitled to if their rent was less than their Local Housing Allowance rate was removed.

- National caps on rates were set at £250, £290, £340 and £400 per week for the one-bedroom, two-bedroom, three-bedroom and four-bedroom rates respectively.

In January 2012, the shared accommodation rule under which rates for claimants aged under 25 are capped at the level of a single room in a shared property, regardless of their actual living situation, was extended to include most single adults without dependent children up to the age of 34, even if they are not living in shared accommodation. All Local Housing Allowance rates are now increased in line with the Consumer Price Index, rather than in line with local rents.

The government expected this package of reforms to save £420 million in 2011-12, £890 million in 2012-13, and £1 billion a year thereafter.[9] Although a total savings figure has yet to be published, an official evaluation concluded that, 'if the reforms had not been introduced, and if [Local Housing Allowance] rates had continued to be linked to median private rents, then overall government expenditure on Housing Benefit over the whole period would have been higher'.[10]

939,220 households were expected to lose an average of £12 a week in Housing Benefit. Although a quarter of affected claimants reported looking for work to try to make up the shortfall in rent money, the official evaluation does not attribute any employment effects to the reforms.[11]

## The Bedroom Tax

The one aspect of the government's welfare reform programme that has attracted most criticism was its decision to dock Housing Benefit from social tenants deemed to be under-occupying their property. The reduction incurred under this penalty is 14% of Housing Benefit for one extra bedroom and 25% for two or more.

Quite why this policy was introduced is a mystery, for it visits onto today's tenants the 'sins' or misjudgements of previous local authorities and their planners, i.e. not enough single bedroom accommodation was built, or the need for it properly anticipated once the surge for single bedroom units was clearly apparent. The first policy objective set out in the impact assessment, carried the government's stated aim: 'The policy is intended to contain Housing Benefit expenditure in the social rented sector'. The impact assessment states that this reform, widely known as the 'bedroom tax', but what the government calls the Spare Room Subsidy, would be expected to deliver savings of £480 million in 2013-14 and £500 million in 2014-15.[12] Yet once it emerged that the policy would miss its target for the first year by £110 million, Esther McVey, the then minister for employment, claimed it was 'never all about saving money' and that it was 'about using the stock, the housing much better'.[13] Even on this front, the bedroom tax failed to deliver. An official evaluation published in July 2014 found that just 5.6% of tenants hit by the bedroom tax downsized; the rest needed to pay the additional monies from their limited resources.[14] The evaluation reported that:

- 57% of affected claimants cut back on what they deemed household essentials.

- 35% cut back on non-essentials in order to pay their shortfall.

- 26% said they had had to borrow money.

Ipsos MORI found in further research that 32% of affected claimants reported having to cut back on food, and 26% on gas and electricity.[15]

Around 550,000 social tenants were affected by the bedroom tax. While the evaluation states that 18% of affected claimants reported either looking for work or seeking to increase their hours, it admits that many struggled to do so, and Ipsos MORI's research suggests just 6% of affected claimants sought work as a direct result of the bedroom tax. Worse still, landlords reported a 16% increase in rent arrears even within the first six months of the bedroom tax coming into force.[16]

A clear lesson here is that the bedroom tax could only ever be workable, or seen to be fair, if there are enough suitable homes to which people can downsize. Without such an option, claimants have been left between a rock and a hard place.

### *How might expenditure be reduced in a fairer way?*

While we address in later chapters the need to boost wages at the bottom, and thereby reduce at least some of the pressure on the Housing Benefit budget, we make a plea here for a proper housebuilding programme to be set in train.

England's public housebuilding budget fell sharply after 2010. It was cut in real terms by £3.6 billion, from £8.8 billion in 2009-10 to £5.2 billion in 2012-13. Despite these cuts the government has delivered minor improvements in the number of new affordable home starts, from 22,000 in 2009-10 to 27,000 in 2013-14. Yet the meaning of affordable housing was changed. The definition of 'affordable' was set at an unprecedented figure of 80% of local private rents. (What we can't report is to what extent this increase in the numbers of affordable homes being built is due to this change in definition.)

The lack of a serious housebuilding programme, together with a rapid increase in the population, has meant that private landlords are able to take advantage of a growing shortage of housing. So while Housing Benefit payments have been cut for 900,000 tenants in the private sector, tenants were left to pick up 90% of the bill.[17] The impact of the cuts, therefore, must have been to widen the gap between renters' incomes and outgoings.

Even if the political will was mustered for a serious housebuilding programme – one that extended beyond brownfield sites and into the scrubbier areas of the sacred green belt – Britain's skills shortage, as things stand, would scupper such a programme. Research from the Local Government Association highlights two alarming trends confronting the government: 10,000 fewer construction qualifications were awarded each year in Britain, while the number of bricklayers required to meet existing, let alone future demand increased by 15,600 between 2013 and 2015.[18]

We propose in our postscript some reforms to sustain the housebuilding programme that Britain so badly needs. We have shown here how vital this will be to any serious attempt at reining in the Housing Benefit budget, in a way which doesn't disadvantage the poorest claimants, including many of those working for low wages.

# iii. Cutting Council Tax Benefit

The government decided in its 2010 Spending Review that local authorities were to administer Council Tax Benefit, but that it would cut the overall budget by 10% (£471 million). And in a sign that this was to be 'localism-lite', the government stipulated to local authorities that pensioners, accounting for 38% of claimants, must retain their full entitlement to benefit. So local authorities effectively had to decide how many of the 3.1 million existing working-age claimants on low incomes were to receive a smaller entitlement, or no benefit at all to help cover the costs of Council Tax.

The outcome, not surprisingly, was grim. The Child Poverty Action Group and the Zacchaeus 2000 Trust found that 2.3 million people on low incomes were on average £167 a year worse off because of this particular cut.[19] Council Tax arrears became one of the fastest growing debt problems encountered by debt charity StepChange – second only to payday loans. In 2010, just 10% of StepChange clients had arrears on their Council Tax bills. In 2014, this had grown to 28%. StepChange reported that 'not only are more of them in arrears, they owe more. Our clients owe an average of £832 in Council Tax arrears – up from £675 in 2010'.[20]

Local authorities, too, found themselves in an impossible position. In March 2014, a year after the introduction of the policy, the total amount of Council Tax outstanding in England reached £2.52 billion; an increase of £152 million on a year earlier.

The total saving to the government from this policy of £471 million, therefore, was yielded not by the Department for Work and Pensions, nor local authorities themselves, but by the Department for Communities and Local Government. As a result, they fell outside the 'welfare savings' bracket, and came with no progress whatsoever towards improving claimants' incentive to work. The government's impact assessment for the policy stated only that 'local authorities may wish to preserve as far as possible the incentive to enter work or to increase earnings'.[21]

# iv. Conclusion

Of the three main reforms the government has introduced to Housing Benefit, therefore, the only one that shows any promise for mending 'broken Britain' is the Benefit Cap, for it is the only one of the three to have shown evidence of improving the incentive for claimants to work. While the bedroom tax and Local Housing Allowance reforms delivered savings to the government, they did so at great cost to respective tenants in the social and private rented sectors and without addressing the real drivers of Housing Benefit expenditure.

One such driver, as we have seen, was the growing numbers of low-paid workers relying on Housing Benefit to top-up their wages to an acceptable minimum that could absorb rent. We have seen also in this chapter how the government restricted some low-income households' entitlement to tax credits and support towards Council Tax bills. It is to the wider developments since 2010, in terms of the numbers and living standards of low-paid workers, that we now turn. In doing so we pose the question: does work provide the best route out of poverty?

The policies we have outlined in this chapter overall will have made this task much more difficult.

# 5

# Work as the best route out of poverty?

## i. The success of Welfare Reform Mark One

The government's overall objective for welfare reform has been to make work pay a higher income than one could expect to receive on benefit, thereby curtailing the welfare dependency of 'broken Britain'. Has this objective been borne out by the data on employment and earnings since 2010?

The government can claim considerable credit for adding to the numbers of people in work. Here is a real success for its welfare-to-work strategy (i.e. Welfare Reform Mark One) and conditionality policies, as well as its cutting of company taxation and the return of a growing economy, but it is important not to overlook the basic instinct of most people who see work as their duty.

Yet, in these favourable circumstances, have the government's policies made work pay a sufficient income? For it is in the success of moving claimants into work that we begin to see the next major challenge to a rolling programme of welfare reform. In a study of those leaving out-of-work benefits between February and March 2011, the Department for Work and Pensions found that 55% of those moving on from Jobseeker's Allowance to work for an employer were employed on either a fixed-term or temporary/casual basis, with respective average earnings of £15,200 and £12,400, and that 25% were back on benefit within seven months.[1] And it is to this group, many of whom are just managing to hold on to their jobs, that the government is proposing to apply sanctions to encourage them to work longer, or to seek jobs with higher pay. Their prospects look grim.

The major challenge, therefore, is how to ensure claimants who were on a low income on benefit are positively helped up the pay scale rather than being parked in low-paying jobs or tipped back onto benefit before they can secure a permanent place in the workforce, or sanctioned for failing to be more successful in finding better paid work.

## ii. The prevalence of poverty

The previous Labour government's assault on pensioner poverty, although expensive, was broadly successful. The poverty rate among pensioners fell from 29.1% in 1996–97 to 18.1% in 2007–08; a fall of 11 percentage points bringing the number of poor pensioners down from 2.9 million to 2 million.

There were no similar signs of success amongst the working-age population. The number of poor childless adults of working age increased under Labour from 3.5 million to 4.2 million, while the number of poor working-age parents remained static at 3.3 million.[2] Little has happened to disturb this dismal record that the government inherited in 2010. Indeed, looking at the data on the numbers of working-age poor, it is difficult to see when or if a general election was held leading to a change in government. 21% of working-age adults were deemed poor in six out of seven years, spanning two of Labour's final three years and each of its successor's first four years in office.[3]

But what of the impact on the poverty data from the government's reform programme since 2010, and in particular its effect on people in low-paid work? The Institute for Fiscal Studies notes over the period between May 2010 and May 2015 that within each income decile, workless households were hit more than three times as hard as equivalent families in work by the government's cuts programme.[4] This will undoubtedly have made work a more attractive proposition to life on benefit.

A notable sign of this strategy bearing fruit is a fall in the total number of people claiming the main out-of-work benefits. This total now stands at its lowest since 1999, down by 975,050 since May 2010 to a total of 3.85 million in November 2014. The number of people living in workless households fell by over 650,000 between 2010 and 2014, and is now the lowest since records began in 1996.[5] With the fall in the overall number of people on benefit so too has there been a fall in the number of children living in households where no one works, down by 388,000 from 1.9 million in May 2010 to 1.5 million in May 2014. However, many of those entering the labour market since 2010 have done so by taking low-paid work.

How successful, therefore, has the government's overall strategy been in ensuring that work is the best route out of poverty? Or have yesterday's workless poor become today's working poor? The government's strategy can be deemed successful on two fronts.

First, the risk of poverty remains much higher in workless households than in families where at least one person is in work. In 2013-14 63% of working-age households in which no adults worked were poor. By contrast only 9% of households in which all adults worked were poor, and likewise 29% of households in which at least one adult was in work.[6] An individual remains much more likely to be poor, therefore, if they are drawing out-of-work benefit. Getting a job cuts dramatically the risk of being poor. The government's welfare reform programme has reinforced this outcome.

Second, the government has increased the gap between the income one could expect to earn from being in work and what they would receive from out-of-work benefit. In the absence of the government's reforms, and had the previous raft of policies remained unchanged, income received through out-of-work benefit would have caught up slightly with earnings. Under this scenario the Institute for Fiscal Studies calculates that benefit income would have increased by 1.7 percentage points, from 55.3% of earned income to 57%, relative to what an individual could expect to receive from work.[7]But the overall impact of the government's reform package so far has been to widen by 2.7 percentage points the gap, termed the 'replacement rate', between what an individual could expect to earn in work and receive in benefit.

The government's reforms therefore have made getting a job an overall more attractive alternative to life on benefit, albeit marginally so. As Table 3 demonstrates, this impact has been particularly pronounced for one-earner couples with no children and single-person households; their replacement rates have been cut respectively by 6.4 percentage points and 2.4 percentage points.

**Table 3:** Impact of the Coalition's reforms on replacement rates

| Group | Replacement rate in 2010 | Replacement rate in 2015 following Coalition reforms | Replacement rate in 2015 without Coalition reforms |
|---|---|---|---|
| Single, no children | 38.7% | 36.3% | 41.5% |
| Lone parent | 70.6% | 70.4% | 72.3% |
| Partner not working, no children | 58.6% | 52.2% | 59.8% |
| Partner not working, children | 70% | 65.6% | 71.8% |
| Partner working, children | 65.6% | 65.8% | 67.3% |
| Partner working, no children | 55% | 54.8% | 56% |
| All households | 55.3% | 53.6% | 57.0% |

Source: Institute for Fiscal Studies, 2013

While this data demonstrates the government's commitment to ensuring people in work are better off than others on out-of-work benefit, it does not tell us whether this income from work is high enough to provide failsafe protection against poverty.

In fact, the shifting composition of the poor since 2010 would suggest that getting a job is not enough, in itself, to fend off poverty. Worryingly from all points of view, working households formed a larger share of the working-age poor in 2014 than they did in 2010; an increase over this period of four percentage points, from 60% in 2009-10 to 64% in 2013-14.[8] How do we account for this growing proportion of working households among Britain's poor?

Here we see the conflict that can arise between the objective of making work pay a sufficient income while at the same time achieving cuts in the welfare budget as part of the government's overall deficit reduction programme, when such a significant part of that welfare budget to be cut has been given over to subsidising low pay – or making work pay a more adequate minimum.

While the increase in the personal tax allowance has incentivised work by reducing the tax burden on the lowest paid, this measure was more than cancelled out by the rest of the government's tax and benefit reforms, including most notably cuts to benefits made available to low-paid workers, such as tax credits and Housing Benefit. The overall impact of the government's reform package on working households has made:[9]

- Single adults fractionally worse off by less than 1%;

- Lone parents 6% worse off;

- One-earner couples with children just under 5% worse off; and

- Two-earner couples with children 2% worse off.

This is hardly a record that shows a discrimination in favour of working families. Real wages also fell, thereby blunting the prospects of making work a more attractive and prosperous alternative to a life on out-of-work benefit. The Institute for Fiscal Studies stated prior to the 2015 general election that falling real wages had halved the impact of the government's reforms to make people in work better off than those on benefit.[10] Wage growth at the bottom, therefore, has been a vital missing part of the government's welfare reform puzzle.

## iii. The wage scene

If we use an absolute threshold for low pay, defined as two thirds of the 2014 median adjusted for Consumer

Price Index (CPI), the proportion of jobs paying low wages halved over the decade leading up to the financial crisis, from 30% (7.59 million) in 1999 to 15% (4.12 million) in 2009. But after 2010 this trend went into reverse, as both the number and proportion increased to 6.08 million and 21% respectively.

The reason why work under the government has not provided failsafe protection against poverty is the very significant growth in the numbers of people in very low-paid jobs, even though many do not now pay tax on their earnings. By 2014, 4.47 million people in work earned less than £10,000, the level to which the personal tax allowance had been raised, compared with 3.83 million in 2010; an increase of just over 640,000 people.

The new earnings profile shows that in 2014, compared with 2010, there were:

- 239,673 more workers earning less than £5,000 a year (in 2014 terms);

- 402,383 more earning between £5,000 and £10,000;

- 457,084 more earning between £10,000 and £15,000;

- 455,675 more earning between £15,000 and £20,000.

This changing shape of the earnings pattern is explained, in part, by the addition of 253,000 jobs in low-paying occupations in 2013-14.

There are, of course, two factors comprising these low earnings. Aside from the rates of hourly pay – the real value of the National Minimum Wage increased in each year prior to 2007 and has fallen a great deal thereafter – a key driver behind the growth in the numbers of workers on low incomes is the restriction many of them face on the number of hours they are able to work. The proportion of part-time workers who, in 2015, said they work part-time because they cannot get more

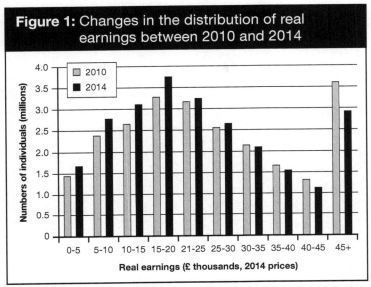

**Figure 1:** Changes in the distribution of real earnings between 2010 and 2014

Source: Office for Budget Responsibility, 2014

hours stood at 1.31 million; an increase of 240,000 since 2010. Similarly, the number of workers employed on zero-hours contracts – contracts that do not guarantee a minimum number of hours from week to week – ballooned under the Coalition to 744,000. Meanwhile the numbers of workers in temporary jobs because they could not find full-time work stood at 589,000 in 2015; 76,000 higher than in 2010. If current rates of employment patterns continue the Trade Union Congress suggests this level of 'under-employment' will not return to its pre-crisis level until at least 2023 – halfway through the next parliament.[11]

Low pay can, for many, all too often become a lifetime curse. The Resolution Foundation looked at the persistence of low pay in 2013.[12] They found that of people who were in low-paid work in April 2002:

- 18% escaped low pay over the next decade (these are the people who were in work and earning above the low pay threshold in April 2010, April 2011 and April 2012);

- 27% were stuck in low pay and unemployment over the next decade (these are the people who only ever held low-paid jobs in the Aprils between 2003 and 2012, including those who moved between unemployment/inactivity and low-paid work);

- 46% cycled out of and into low pay over the next decade (these are the people who escaped low pay at some point during the decade, but did not escape out of low pay for good, as they were not in higher-paid work for April 2010, April 2011 and April 2012).

But looking only at employees would leave us with an incomplete picture, such has been the growth in self-employment since 2010. Recent developments in the numbers of people classing themselves as self-employed have sparked some debate as to whether our labour market has begun delivering entrepreneur after entrepreneur, or that there is a troubling tide of insecurity at the bottom. In short, there is some truth in both accounts.

The number of people classing themselves as self-employed reached a record high in 2014, growing by half a million since 2010 to 4.52 million. Moreover, the number of self-employed identifying themselves as managers and directors increased from 502,000 in the last year of the previous Labour government to 739,000 in 2014. Likewise the number of self-employed workers in other 'professional occupations' rose from 627,000 in Labour's final year in office to 748,000 in 2014. Almost one in six workers now class themselves as self-employed. If this growth persists at the rate it has since 2008, the number of self-employed people will outstrip those working in public sector jobs by 2018.[13]

Why, therefore, did self-employed workers' median incomes shrink in real terms by £29 a week in 2012-13, having already declined by £65 a week between 2007-08 and 2011-12? We believe the answer is to be found in the rapid increase in the number of self-employed workers in lower-paying industries. For the number of workers identifying themselves as self-employed in care, leisure and other service occupations increased by almost a third under the Coalition government, from 243,000 to 311,000, as did those in sales and other customer service jobs, from 81,000 to 105,000, and elementary occupations, from 206,000 to 286,000.[14] These trends might help to explain why around a third of the self-employed report incomes below the personal allowance.[15]

# iv. Conclusion

Real wage growth at the bottom has been the missing piece of the government's welfare reform puzzle. While work remains preferable to a life on benefit and brings with it a dramatic reduction in the risk of being poor, and the government's efforts have reinforced this outcome, it does not provide complete protection against poverty. As we have seen, in previous chapters as well as this one, the explanation for the government's failure to enshrine work as a failsafe means of guarding against poverty is twofold. First, there has been a significant increase in the number of people moving from low benefit income into low-paid jobs and being parked there; second, cuts have been imposed upon benefits and tax credits claimed by this same group of low-paid workers.

At a time of falling real wages and the growth of low-paid work, therefore, the onus would fall upon the government's flagship welfare reform, Universal Credit, to fix 'broken Britain' by enshrining work as the best route out of poverty. It is to this task we now turn our attention.

# 6

## Universal Credit: 'Welfare That Works'?

### i. The changing profile of claimant dependency

Central to the Centre for Social Justice's analysis of 'broken Britain' was what it saw as a benefits system that discriminated against work. To mend 'broken Britain' required a transformation of the benefit system by way of the introduction of Universal Credit. The political historians may be interested in how a programme, so full of risk and potentially at such great cost, came to be the Coalition's flagship welfare reform policy with so little public and maybe cabinet debate. Our concern again here is in the record of its implementation, coverage and cost.

Universal Credit was unveiled in a 2010 White Paper entitled 'Welfare That Works'. All too soon the government trumpeted it as the means through which benefits would be simplified and work made more attractive. A third promise was that it would help bring benefit expenditure under control. Yet the early findings from Universal Credit's glacial rollout suggest that each of these three goals face considerable difficulties in being achieved.

The assumptions underpinning Universal Credit were laid out in a series of CSJ reports beginning with

'Breakdown Britain' in 2006. These assumptions were taken into government by Iain Duncan Smith and, not surprisingly, many of his statements on Universal Credit echo what the CSJ wrote in these reports. Upon setting sail into these uncharted waters of Universal Credit, Duncan Smith proclaimed that, 'we need reform that tackles the underlying problem of welfare dependency'. But dependency, as we have seen in all its three forms, has continued since 2010 – not only amongst claimants in and out of work, but also amongst employers benefiting from a burgeoning wage subsidy coming from the tax credit system, which in 2013 met 4% of Britain's wage bill, and landlords for whom Housing Benefit has provided an ever-growing source of revenue.

Following Labour's three terms in office, the profile of claimant dependency had taken a different form where it was primarily families in low-paid work rather than those who were out of work. Table 4 shows that in August 1999, the month from which we have consistent data, 786,000 working-age claimants were registered for in-work benefit, compared with 5 million claiming out-of-work benefits.

**Table 4:** Numbers of in- and out-of-work households claiming benefit in 1999, 2010, and 2014

| Year | 1999 | 2010 | 2014 |
|---|---|---|---|
| Numbers out of work and on benefit | 5 million | 4.8 million | 3.8 million |
| Numbers in work and on benefit | 0.78 million | 4.8 million | 3.2 million |

Source: House of Commons Library

Eleven years later, and following Labour's welfare-to-work programmes and the unheralded expansion of the tax credit system, the numbers claiming out-of-work benefit had fallen to 4.8 million – a decrease of 3.3% –

but this total in 2010 was matched by the numbers of low-paid workers claiming benefit, the army of whom had increased in size by 515% to 4.8 million. The government's reform programme by the end of 2014 had reduced both counts respectively, to 3.8 million and 3.2 million, leaving in place a smaller but nonetheless substantial army of in- and out-of-work claimants.

## ii. Claimants' marginal tax rates

How then does this army fare under the current tax and benefit system, as it stands in 2015? We have seen how the government reinforced the gap between what one could expect to receive from work and on benefit. But what of the transition into work and the prospects of improving one's income once in work? We can summarise the existing system as follows:

- People receiving tax credits, but paying no Income Tax or National Insurance, pay a marginal tax rate of 41p in the pound.

- People receiving tax credits, and paying Income Tax and National Insurance, pay a marginal tax rate of 73p in the pound.

- People receiving Housing Benefit and tax credits, but paying no Income Tax or National Insurance, pay a marginal tax rate of 79p in the pound.

- People receiving Housing Benefit and tax credits, and paying Income Tax and National Insurance, pay a marginal tax rate of 91p in the pound; this increases to 96p once Council Tax support is factored in.

And what of their fortunes under Universal Credit? The headline figure suggests a marginal improvement under Universal Credit where many claimants entering work would see their benefit withdrawn not at 73p or more in the pound under the current medley of means-tested benefits, but at a rate at least 8p lower, at 65p in the pound.[1]

The full picture, however, is much more complex. The new single benefit withdrawal rate of 65p in the pound will lead to higher marginal tax rates for some claimants, and lower for others, depending on the combination of benefits and tax credits in play:

- People receiving tax credits, but paying no Income Tax or National Insurance, are likely to be substantially worse off to the tune of 24p in the pound under Universal Credit.

- People receiving tax credits, and paying Income Tax and National Insurance, are likely to be worse off by 3p in the pound.

- People receiving Housing Benefit and tax credits, but paying no Income Tax or National Insurance, are likely to be better off under Universal Credit, by 14p in the pound.

- People receiving Housing Benefit and tax credits, and paying Income Tax and National Insurance, are likely to be at least 26p in the pound better off under Universal Credit.

The government summarised in its impact assessment the effect of Universal Credit on these marginal tax rates:[2]

- There would now be virtually no households paying marginal tax rates above 80p in the pound.

- 1.3 million fewer claimants would pay marginal tax rates of 70p or more in the pound.

- Although these ginormous rates are all but abolished, 600,000 more people would see their overall marginal tax rates increase rather than decrease.

- Working households who are currently in receipt of tax credits will pay a marginal tax rate of 76p after Income Tax and National Insurance, which is 3p higher than under the current system.

Further analysis by the Institute for Fiscal Studies found in 2011 that, compared with the current system, 350,000 more claimants would pay marginal tax rates of 60p or more in the pound.[3] This group comprises mainly second earners in a couple who under the current system lose 41p in the pound on earnings below £8,060. An all too typical situation, in which the 65p rate imposed under Universal Credit represents an effective tax rise of 24p on this group of claimants, is laid bare by the Resolution Foundation; a second earner who gets a job paying £10,600 would see their net household income rise by £6,000 under the current system, falling to just £3,600 under Universal Credit.[4]

Whether a reduction in the marginal tax rate will transform claimants' dependency on welfare will be questionable to most people, particularly when so much of the political debate centres on the excessive marginal tax rate of 45% for earners at the top of the income pile. This judgement is of course theoretical. Any reduction in the marginal tax rate will only come for particular groups of Universal Credit claimants should the benefit be introduced, but then, the failure of Universal Credit to encompass also Council Tax support and free school meals will throw all of these calculations into a mild chaos, to put it at its gentlest.

Universal Credit as it is being introduced is not the Universal Credit that was promised. The stated objective was for Universal Credit to replace all means-tested benefits which both working and non-working households currently claim. But after much bargaining the Universal Credit now being constructed does not cover Council Tax support. Universal Credit claimants in work will apply separately for Council Tax support which is being administered by local authorities. While each could decide its own means-test, most authorities have adopted IT systems that withdraw Council Tax support at 20%, giving an eye wateringly high marginal tax rate facing Universal Credit claimants. The highest rate (30%) set by some local authorities in England is double the lowest (15%).[5]

Likewise the marginal tax rate was destined originally to be set at 55p in the pound. The government opted instead for a rate of 65p.

Moreover the work allowance – the level of earnings at which this marginal tax rate begins to be applied – was reformed in the 2015 Summer Budget. This latest reform, which passed through parliament in November 2015:

- Abolished the work allowance for childless workers;

- Reduced the work allowance to £4,764 for claimants who will not receive help towards housing costs – a reduction of £4,044 for lone parents and £1,686 for couples with children;

- Reduced the work allowance to £2,304 for claimants who will receive help towards housing costs – a reduction of £852 for lone parents and £360 for couples with children.

Of those low-paid workers who make a new claim for Universal Credit, and who do not receive help with housing costs:

- Childless workers will be £866 worse off compared with what they would have got under the current system;

- Lone parents will be £2,629 worse off;
- Couples with children will be £1,084 worse off.

Of those low-paid workers who receive help with housing costs under Universal Credit:

- Childless workers will be £866 worse off compared with what they would have got under the current system;
- Lone parents will be £554 worse off;
- Couples with children will be £234 worse off.

The overarching goal of Universal Credit – of reducing the marginal tax rate for the working poor – has not been met. 'Broken Britain' will not be mended by the introduction of this benefit. Furthermore, Universal Credit was built on the faulted assumption that any increase in income, no matter how small, would revolutionise work incentives for claimants who have come to view their unearned benefit as a pension. Work for this group has to show a very substantial increase in their income if they are freely to seek work.

## iii. The costs and implementation of Universal Credit

So what of the costs and rollout of Universal Credit? The June 2010 Spending Review allocated £2 billion over four years, both to set up Universal Credit and to ensure claimants would not be worse off once they started claiming, with a view to all claimants on existing benefits being migrated to the new benefit by 2017. To achieve this target, let alone secure the target of the transformation to a new system, it was important to stop recruiting at some stage new claimants onto those existing benefits that Universal Credit is intended to replace. The plans were clear. There were meant to have been no new claims for Jobseeker's Allowance, Employment and Support Allowance, Income Support, Working and Child Tax Credits or Housing Benefit from April 2014.[6] That this target has not been met is solely because of the failure of the government to deliver Universal Credit on anything like its original timetable. As shown in Table 5, 3.63 million new claimants have continued to be recruited onto this existing range of out-of-work benefits.

**Table 5:** Number of new claims to the main out-of-work benefits between April 2014 and June 2015

| Year | New claims between April 2014 and June 2015 |
| --- | --- |
| Income Support | 194,310 |
| Employment and Support Allowance | 686,740 |
| Jobseeker's Allowance | 2,753,418 |
| Total | 3,634,468 |

Source: House of Commons Library

Let us therefore take a more detailed look at Universal Credit's rollout. In April 2013, the government began to pilot Universal Credit in four jobcentres in the north-west of England. They were limited to new claims from single people in the simplest of circumstances – unemployed with no children. The national implementation was billed to begin for all new claimants from October 2013. Yet, as Table 6 shows, events haven't gone to plan. It is as though a space programme that was aiming for Mars found itself heading for the Earth's moon.

**Table 6:** Changes to Universal Credit rollout assumption, November 2015[7]

| Average caseloads (millions) | 2014-15 | 2015-16 | 2016-17 | 2017-18 | 2018-19 | 2019-20 | 2020-21 |
|---|---|---|---|---|---|---|---|
| March 2013 assumption | 1.66 | 4.46 | 6.09 | 7.17 | 7.39 | | |
| December 2013 assumption | 0.03 | 0.36 | 2.89 | 5.77 | 6.62 | | |
| December 2014 DWP | 0.02 | 0.17 | 1.49 | 3.99 | 5.69 | 6.71 | |
| December 2014 OBR | 0.02 | 0.17 | 0.67 | 2.94 | 4.92 | 6.29 | |
| July 2015 assumption | 0.02 | 0.10 | 0.60 | 2.20 | 4.10 | 5.40 | 6.10 |
| November 2015 DWP | 0.02 | 0.10 | 0.30 | 1.40 | 3.30 | 5.00 | 6.20 |
| November 2015 OBR | 0.02 | 0.10 | 0.30 | 1.40 | 3.30 | 4.80 | 5.80 |

Source: Office for Budget Responsibility

There have been four major adjustments to the start date of Universal Credit. The first four pilots began in April 2013 and it was forecast that the follow-through would be such that there would be 1.66 million people claiming Universal Credit in 2014-15. The government missed this target by a total of 1.64 million. Instead of 1.66 million claiming Universal Credit as planned by December 2014, the total was 22,900.

The government predicted in March 2013 that there would be 4.46 million claiming Universal Credit in 2015-16. The actual number in July 2015 was a mere 75,427 registered claimants (although this doesn't confirm they were receiving benefit), 4.38 million short of the projected total for that date.

But Iain Duncan Smith remains confident that at some stage and at some unnamed date in the future, the promises of Universal Credit will be fulfilled. A saving grace has been a reduction in the costs of introducing the scheme – not surprisingly. Of the £2 billion set aside by the chancellor in 2010 to cover the costs of rolling out Universal Credit, more than two thirds remained unspent by the end of 2014.

Missing the deadlines by miles for the number of claimants who should be receiving Universal Credit hasn't dented the government's enthusiasm for setting equally ambitious targets for the future. The latest guesstimates for the transfer of existing claimants onto the new Universal Credit is 'after 2017'. How much after 2017 the government doesn't wish to divulge. Nor does it disclose how many will have been transferred before then. It is equally vague about by when the bulk of claimants will have been transferred. It looks, however, as though it will be quite some time after 2017. The Office for Budget Responsibility, which considers the introduction of Universal Credit as it impacts upon future social security costs, has stated that it expects tax credit claims to continue in their current form until 2018-19.[8] It wisely does not speculate how much longer beyond that date it might take to transfer all those then in receipt of tax credits to Universal Credit.

For the scheme to deliver its claimed potential it is necessary not only for it to be rolled out. Universal Credit depends crucially on this month's benefit being linked to last month's earnings. For this to be achieved Universal Credit relies on the real-time information (RTI) system being supplied by a very considerable number of employers to Her Majesty's Revenue and Customs (HMRC). This information is then transferred to the

Department for Work and Pensions to calculate Universal Credit. This information is central to the department being able accurately to pay a claimant their monthly entitlement. A big attraction of Universal Credit has been billed that current payments will be varied according to the income registered during the previous month. Without this automatic link to the immediate period of earnings claimants will begin to be paid incorrect sums in Universal Credit. These over- and under-payments will then land Universal Credit into the same mire that many tax credit claimants find themselves with all too often having large overpayments being presented to them for repayment. This is not a minor issue. By 2013 the total outstanding amount owed to HMRC in tax credit overpayments had reached £5.6 billion. The debt was shared among 4.7 million families.[9]

So far the RTI system hasn't fully lived up to its billing on this front either. We've encountered not insubstantial concerns among small businesses about whether their systems will be able to cope with RTI and its accompanying requirements. The National Audit Office informed us in February 2014 that while the vast majority of British industry was signed up to RTI, 2,952 small and medium enterprises and 156,000 'micro-businesses' employing fewer than 10 employees were not yet using the system. This group of micro-businesses was granted an opt-out period until April 2016. What's more, the Department for Work and Pensions did not yet know how many small businesses, those that employ between 10 and 49 workers, had taken up the option of its temporary RTI opting-out period, which had been in place since April 2013.

Many smaller businesses make frequent payments and payroll adjustments over the course of an average month, and each of these triggers the need to report to HMRC any changes in circumstances. Indeed most people on low incomes will be much more familiar with receiving their wages on a weekly basis than at the end of each month, even if the pattern is changing. Any burden from Universal Credit might be expected to be greater on those businesses that lack the infrastructure of larger companies.

The problems of Universal Credit do not end here, however. Other government departments have highlighted problems in respect of the Department for Work and Pensions' flagship policy. Officials at HMRC are said to have identified claimants who are underreporting their actual earnings, and are now looking at introducing six-monthly reporting to prevent the potential for employers and employees colluding to maximise their benefit payment.[10] So much for the claim made in 2010 that Universal Credit would remove the incentive to defraud the taxpayer.[11]

Another of the government's great hopes for Universal Credit – that it would bring greater simplicity and clarity to the maze of means-tests – is in danger of being undermined by what has not been included under the Universal Credit banner.

## iv. Much pain and not much gain

The government's failure to set out whether children living in households in receipt of Universal Credit would be entitled to free school meals has muddied the waters still further in respect of work incentives and remains to the detriment of poor children. Under the current system, even following the introduction of universal free school meals for under-8s, 1.6 million children from poorer families are disqualified from receiving free school meals because their parents are in work, even though they are on low income. If their parents were to receive the same level of income (below £16,190 a year) but were not in work, their family would save £400 a year thanks to the free school meal scheme for families on out-of-work benefits. But, as things stand, these children will continue to lose out, and their parents will be penalised for working for their poverty, as the government has repeatedly failed to clarify whether Universal Credit would bring with it automatic entitlement to free school meals.

Likewise, the government took simplification to the point of absurdity by abolishing Council Tax Benefit and devolving responsibility to local authorities for compensating households on low income with their Council Tax bills. Life is 'made simpler' for the Universal Credit applications and calculations certainly, but only at the price the claimant pays in the loss of income. As we have seen each local authority is free to set its own criteria and taper rates for Council Tax support. But with less money being given to them than what the projected Council Tax Benefit budget entailed, most local authorities short of overall funds have had to restrict eligibility for, and not exempt any household income when deciding the level of, Council Tax support. It has been estimated that this move alone will increase the marginal tax rate facing people claiming Universal Credit, on average, by 7p in the pound.[12] This would bring the true marginal deduction rate to 72%. The CSJ proposed in 2009 that support for Council Tax bills be kept within the Universal Credit tent. Duncan Smith took this proposal into office, but it was in fact vetoed in the 2010 Spending Review.

One issue has, however, been settled in favour of some Universal Credit claimants – should they ever find themselves able to register. The government announced that from April 2016 it would increase childcare support within Universal Credit to better incentivise work and ensure that it is worthwhile for low- and middle-income parents to work up to full-time hours. An additional £200 million of support for childcare will be provided, and it is hoped that this sum will cover 85% of childcare costs for all households should they qualify for the Universal Credit childcare element.

# v. Conclusion

Universal Credit has failed the test set for it by the reformers within the government of fixing 'broken Britain' by 'making welfare work'. As things stand, tax credits look set to remain the major wage subsidy.

One consequence of the government's failure to deliver Universal Credit, and the substantial savings it was meant to have released, was to make that much more significant the need for reform elsewhere within the existing stock of benefits. This reform would be necessary for the government to achieve its planned cutbacks in the working-age welfare budget, encourage claimants into work, and thereby fix 'broken Britain'. Hence the urgency with which it set about reforming Incapacity Benefit, and it is to this effort we now turn.

# 7

## Dividing the sheep and the goats?

### i. Reforming Incapacity Benefit

For well over three decades successive governments have wrestled to control the growing costs of Incapacity Benefit. 'To ease the passing'[1] of the loss of largely male, moderately well-paid jobs became the government's strategy to maintain social peace when negotiating a rapid rundown of Britain's heavy industries. As redundancies in these industries moved from a trickle to a flood, peace was bought by the offer of more generous Incapacity Benefit payments (then called Invalidity Benefit) over the value of Unemployment Benefit (as Jobseeker's Allowance was then called). Invalidity Benefit had an additional advantage over the payment of means-tested Unemployment Benefit; it was paid irrespective of a partner's earnings, thereby enhancing the possibility of increasing a household's overall income.

This social peace strategy came with a price tag, however, and a growing one at that. The numbers of what were initially redundant workers claiming Incapacity Benefit rose substantially; more than trebling from 796,000 in 1983 to a staggering 2.49 million by 1996. The annual costs rose accordingly, ballooning from £5.1 billion in 1983 to £11.4 billion in real terms by 1996.

Once the fear of disorder that might have followed these mass redundancies had abated, successive governments changed direction. Government efforts moved to curtailing entitlement and thereby cutting the cost of Incapacity Benefit. These efforts centred on making new claimants' access to benefit that much more difficult by raising the eligibility bar.

This process of making the gateways to benefit that much more difficult to negotiate began under the previous Labour government. In 2008 Labour introduced Employment and Support Allowance, thereby heralding the replacement of Incapacity Benefit and Income Support for claimants with disabilities. The test for Employment and Support Allowance became a Work Capability Assessment which diverted those found capable of some form of work to Jobseeker's Allowance, and those who might one day be helped into this position to the Work Related Activity Group of Employment and Support Allowance. Others whose health prevented them from any form of working were placed into the Support Group of Employment and Support Allowance. Existing claimants of Incapacity Benefit under Labour's plans were due to be moved onto Employment and Support Allowance between October 2010 and April 2014. This was the programme that Iain Duncan Smith inherited.

The Labour government became frustrated in its attempts to reduce the number of claimants by its Work Capability Assessment and it did not take long for the Coalition to share this response. Progress was painfully slow with the number of people claiming Employment and Support Allowance or Incapacity Benefit falling only from 2.42 million in 2009-10 to 2.38 million in 2014-15. Of the 1.38 million Incapacity Benefit claims that had been reassessed between October 2010 and March 2014, only 253,560 had been found fit for work and transferred to Jobseeker's Allowance. The figure forecast for 2015-16 in the June 2010 Budget for the number of working-age claimants of incapacity benefits was put at 2.17 million. Yet in the 2014 Autumn Statement, the government was forecasting that there would be 2.52 million such claimants in 2015-16 – up by a third of a million claimants.

Not surprisingly the expected savings of around £1 billion from reassessing Incapacity Benefit claimants by 2014-15 that had been forecast back in 2010 had to be cut by almost three quarters – down to £281 million.[2] Worse news in respect of the benefit savings target was to come. The Office for Budget Responsibility in June 2015 revised upwards the forecast for Employment and Support Allowance/Incapacity Benefit expenditure on the grounds that even fewer claimants than the radically revised total would be expected to be found fit for work.[3] The reason why these savings have not been forthcoming can be found in the falling number of Incapacity Benefit claimants found fit for some kind of work.

In 2009, the first year in which claimants were assessed for their capability to look for work, and the final full year of the previous Labour government, 63% of people first assessed were found fit for work with 26% asked to undertake some work-related activity. Only 10% were found entitled to unconditional support. The latest figures show just how dramatically the estimated savings had to be revised. By 2013 just 34% were found fit for work and 47% were given unconditional support. The remainder – some 19% – were assessed as having limited capability to undertake some work-related activities, such as an occasional interview with a Jobcentre Plus official.

**Table 7:** Outcomes for claimants tested for Employment and Support Allowance

| Year | Proportion of claimants found as being capable of work | Proportion of claimants found as being capable of some work-related activity | Proportion of claimants found incapable of work |
|------|---------|---------|---------|
| 2009 | 63% | 26% | 10% |
| 2013 | 34% | 19% | 47% |

Source: DWP Statistical Releases

A further source of frustration for the government was the delayed timetable for reassessing the remainder of current Incapacity Benefit claims. The process of moving people off Incapacity Benefit and onto Employment and Support Allowance or Jobseeker's Allowance was meant to have been completed by April 2014. But just a month prior to this date 102,000 claimants were still awaiting reassessment. The Department for Work and Pensions forecast eight months later, in December 2014, that 85,000 people would still be on Incapacity Benefit in 2015-16 – up to two years after the shutters were to come down on payments to anyone claiming Incapacity Benefit.

The government focused its frustration over the failure to close Incapacity Benefit to new claimants at Atos, the private contractor entrusted by the Labour government with the reassessment process. The boiling over of the government's frustration was plain for all to see when Atos was sacked in 2015.[4] Mike Penning, the then minister overseeing the migration to the new benefit, said, upon terminating the contract, that the reports produced by Atos contained 'significant quality failures', adding with some considerable glee that 'Atos will not receive a single penny of compensation from the taxpayer for the early termination of their contract.' Comfort, no doubt, in dispensing with Atos's work. No such comfort on the benefit costs front, however.

We can see from this brief overview why the Office for Budget Responsibility decided to rank spending on Incapacity Benefit and Employment and Support Allowance as the most significant risk affecting its forecast for future welfare expenditure, the others being Personal Independence Payment and Universal Credit, outlined in Table 8.

**Table 8:** Risks to welfare expenditure forecasts, identified in June 2015 by the Office for Budget Responsibility

| Benefit | Risk factor |
| --- | --- |
| Incapacity Benefit/ Employment and Support Allowance | • Backlog of Work Capability Assessments for existing Incapacity Benefit claimants<br>• Higher than expected proportion of claimants found entitled to unconditional support |
| Disability Living Allowance/Personal Independence Payment | • Slower than planned transition from DLA to PIP<br>• Higher than expected proportion of claimants found entitled to PIP |
| Universal Credit | • Repeatedly delayed rollout |

Source: Office for Budget Responsibility, *Welfare Trends Report*, June 2015

The government had set about implementing Labour's proposed reassessment programme so it could begin making inroads into the working-age welfare budget. Neither Labour nor the Coalition since 2010 can be faulted for their efforts on this front. But the many difficulties arising from its implementation, and the subsequent changes the government introduced to try to repair some of these faults in the process, have blunted such prospects.

To what extent, though, could this frustration be attributed to the actual design of the reassessment process? Is a one-off Work Capability Assessment the most appropriate means through which an individual's readiness, or otherwise, for work can be determined? With so much riding on this single event, and with often complex physical and mental health issues in play, decisions have always been open to dispute.

How might the government, therefore, more effectively help claimants into a position where they feel able to prepare themselves for some sort of work? One such remedy might be to reform the Work Capability Assessment into a longer-term process, thereby leaving behind what could be described as an unreliable and unsympathetic examination under the current system. A more gradual test could determine benefit eligibility through a regular set of appointments, in which those conducting the reassessment can get a better idea of the factors that may enhance or limit a claimant's ability to look for some sort of work.

Resulting from this process could be an 'improving your life' contract, bestowing upon claimants some basic duties they have a realistic chance of being able to fulfil. Listed alongside these duties would be the help they can draw upon to fulfil them. This help might consist of frequent meetings with a specialist health adviser, for example.

But whatever help is deemed appropriate for an individual claimant, it would be provided on the basis that it should support their efforts to find some sort of work.

## ii. Replacing Disability Living Allowance with Personal Independence Payment

Whereas reducing the number of Incapacity Benefit claims was a shared endeavour of both Labour and the current government, the move to reduce the cost of Disability Living Allowance claims arose solely after 2010. Disability Living Allowance is a tax-free benefit designed to help disabled people with mobility and care costs.

When Labour took office in 1997 there were 1.84 million people claiming Disability Living Allowance. Disability Living Allowance found itself exempt from reform throughout Labour's time in office. The numbers claiming the unreformed Disability Living Allowance climbed to 3.13 million in 2010, with the costs over this period increasing similarly in real terms from £6.69 billion in 1996-97 to £12.73 billion in 2009-10.

Reforming Disability Living Allowance had never before made it onto the political agenda. Prior to 2010 the growth in spending on Disability Living Allowance, as well as the numbers of people claiming, was largely absent from the political debate on welfare reform. The prospect of reforming Disability Living Allowance was totally absent from each of the main parties' 2010 manifestos. Hence the surprise which greeted the government's decision in 2011 to completely replace Disability Living Allowance for new claimants from April 2013 with a new Personal Independence Payment.

Personal Independence Payment is similar in structure to Disability Living Allowance, comprising a daily living component and a mobility component. Claimants qualify by filling in a self-assessment form. However, under Personal Independence Payment, unlike Disability Living Allowance, a claimant's eligibility then is dependent on their disability being assessed at a medical. But it is a medical with a difference. And here is the second significant change. The disability test for Personal Independence Payment involves an assessment of the ability of an individual to 'participate fully in society' rather than of the severity of their impairment. This means that, unlike in Disability Living Allowance, there are no medical conditions that will lead to an automatic entitlement to Personal Independence Payment; it is, however, a medical test that determines eligibility and the value of Personal Independence Payment. While the government did not set out what it means to 'participate fully', the daily living component of Personal Independence Payment is available to claimants who have difficulty eating, washing, dressing and undressing, reading and communicating, managing medicines and treatment, making financial decisions, and meeting new people.

Second, the mobility component is allocated on the basis of a claimant's ability to plan and follow a journey, rather than a simple assessment of their ability to walk unaided. Personal Independence Payment also involves an objective and continuing assessment of claimants' needs. And, just as there are no medical conditions that will lead to an automatic enrolment, there are no lifetime awards either. Each claim is assessed and requires renewal after a set period of time. The assumption is that the Personal Independence Payment will be awarded for a fixed term of between a year and ten years, rather than being awarded for life. Claimants will automatically be reassessed at the end of this term, as well as during that term if circumstances change. In order to make a claim, an individual is required to submit a form detailing the effect their disability has on their day-to-day life, along with documentation and/or references from medical professionals and carers.

By April 2015 a total of 950,700 applications had been made for Personal Independence Payment and decisions had been made on 810,500 of these claims, leaving 140,200 claims outstanding.[5] Within the total number of applications there were 136,700 reassessments of existing Disability Living Allowance claimants; 814,000 were new claims. 77% of existing Disability Living Allowance claimants were found eligible for Personal Independence Payment, as were 50% of new claimants.

People being moved from Disability Living Allowance continue to receive their existing payments until a decision has been made on their entitlement to Personal Independence Payment. A first Personal Independence Payment is meant to arrive 28 days after this decision, although the Department for Work and Pensions is unable to tell us whether this works out in practice.

Mystery also shrouds the financial position of new Personal Independence Payment applicants who weren't previously claiming Disability Living Allowance. The department again holds no data on new claimants' sources of income while their application is being processed. This process takes weeks, and often months.

Disability Living Allowance remains open to new claims and the numbers of people claiming the benefit rose slightly in the last parliament, from 3.13 million in 2009-10 to 3.34 million in 2013-14. Expenditure rose likewise in real terms from £12.73

billion to £14.09 billion, which led the Office for Budget Responsibility to conclude in June 2015 that expenditure on disability benefits in 2014-15 would be £600 million higher than expected.[6] Eventually the move to Personal Independence Payment and the smaller caseload is expected to reduce spending by £2.4 billion a year by 2019-20. Time will tell whether this estimate is any more accurate than it has been for expenditure on other benefits.

The government forecast in 2010 that introducing assessments under the new Personal Independence Payment regime would save £360 million in 2013-14, rising to around £1 billion in 2014-15. The Office for Budget Responsibility stated in October 2014 that it did not expect any of these savings to arrive before the 2015 election.[7]

Why, therefore, did the substitution of Personal Independence Payment for Disability Living Allowance fail to deliver these savings? Our answer is simple; there were fewer people claiming Personal Independence Payment, and more claiming Disability Living Allowance, which it was supposed to have replaced by the end of the last parliament. The impact assessment accompanying the introduction of Personal Independence Payment assumed that there would be 1.7 million people of working age claiming Personal Independence Payment and nobody receiving Disability Living Allowance in 2015-16.[8] The government's most recent estimate in June 2015 suggests there will be just 476,000 working-age Personal Independence Payment claimants in 2015-16 and a further 1.48 million receiving Disability Living Allowance – bringing the total number of working-age claimants in receipt of disability benefits to 1.96 million.[9]

We welcome the introduction of Personal Independence Payment but, again, given its glacial rollout very little has changed on this welfare front. What, then, of the initiatives that have delivered successfully on the government's objectives?

# 8

# Big successes

## i. Success in cutting overall welfare expenditure

The Coalition achieved something that no other government has been able to. The reforms enacted since 2010 resulted in a real-terms cut in working-age welfare expenditure in the last parliament.

The single area where we report success without qualification for the government in achieving its welfare objectives is in delivering its plan to cut the welfare bill over and above what it was projected to be. Key to this delivery has been the reform to the indexation of working-age benefits and tax credits.

In 2011-12 and 2012-13, tax credits and benefits for working-age claimants (including disability benefits) were indexed to the Consumer Price Index (CPI). CPI tends to increase more slowly than both Retail Price Index (RPI) and the Rossi index (RPI without housing costs). The Rossi Index prior to April 2011 was the formula used to uprate means-tested benefits. In terms of savings this seemingly innocuous move reduced the welfare bill, compared to what it would otherwise have been, by £4.3 billion.[1] It therefore accounts for the most significant change enacted in the last parliament. Further savings of £1.7 billion were pursued by capping benefit increases at 1% for three years from April 2013 (disability benefits are excluded) – although even this measure looks likely to have saved £1 billion less than forecast in the 2013 Budget. Additional savings of £3 billion were sought through freezing Child Benefit and Working Tax Credit. It is important to remember that this package comes on top of the not insubstantial cuts to Housing Benefit and Council Tax support. Hence why the government's endeavour to achieve savings lies beyond doubt.

There is a downside, however, in that this policy comes with a cost in terms of cuts in claimants' real living standards and also in an increase in child poverty. The government has estimated that its reforms to the indexation of benefits and tax credits will have resulted in around an extra 200,000 children being made poor by 2015-16, and the differential rates of inflation faced by poorer families will have been compounded by cash freezes and minimal annual increases in benefit income.

The government had hoped that by the end of the last parliament the package of measures enacted since 2010 would have reduced the overall welfare budget in 2015 by a net total of £19 billion, compared with what an unreformed system would have cost. According to one recent calculation by the Institute for Fiscal Studies, the net effect of the government's welfare reform programme was to meet £16.7 billion of this total by 2015-16.[2]

Explaining the 'missing' £2.3 billion of the £19 billion target for savings is one of our easier tasks. The first explanation lies in the government's decision to afford protection to all pensioners, whatever their means, who as a group have been and will continue to increase as a proportion of the overall population. The Office for National Statistics forecasts a 31% increase in the number of pensioners between 2012 and 2037 – almost three times the expected growth in the working-age population (12%).[3] Pensioners' benefits are uprated by either 2.5%, CPI inflation, or the annual increase in average earnings, in a formula known as the 'triple lock'.

The Institute for Fiscal Studies notes that the consequences of this protection afforded in the last parliament by the government resulted in a real terms increase in the annual pensioners' welfare bill of 1.2%, while annual real-terms expenditure on working-age welfare fell by 1.4% each year. Annual spending on pensioner benefits increased by a real-terms average of £300 per pensioner, regardless of their means.[4] Here we can see how the government's protection policy reinforced a trend apparent under Labour which has resulted in pensioners' incomes moving from being 20% behind the rest of the population in 1992, and 5% behind in 2008, to a position where the typical pensioner is now better off than the typical non-pensioner.[5]

A second part of the answer is that some of the savings promised in the early days of the Coalition have yet to materialise. Time-limiting contributory Employment and Support Allowance, for example, is only saving half of what the government claimed for it. The June 2010 Spending Review anticipated savings of £2 billion a year by 2014-15, yet this later was revised downwards to £1 billion.[6] The House of Commons Library estimates that the government spent over £10 billion more on Housing Benefit over the last parliament than it was forecasting in November 2010.[7] The government overspent likewise on incapacity benefits by £8.5 billion and on disability benefits by £1.7 billion. Such overspends necessitated other measures taken throughout the last parliament – on the indexation of working-age benefits, for example – to rein in expenditure.

A third part of our explanation for the non-delivery of expected benefit savings lies in the upward pressure applied to the working-age welfare budget by the high rents and low wages that have characterised the housing and labour markets since 2010.

There is a fourth reason why the cuts in the welfare bill have not been achieved as was estimated, and here lies a problem that is going to feature much more prominently in the 2015 parliament. We are referring to the government's failure to implement its two flagship reforms to the structure of working-age benefits – Universal Credit and Personal Independence Payment.

The reformers' vision for welfare had relied in a not insignificant way on the rolling out of Universal Credit and for this to be the great agent incentivising work. Yet it has been beset by delays and, as we record elsewhere in this audit, might not even be fully rolled out a decade after it was first announced. Universal Credit was meant to have been saving money in the working-age welfare budget – a cool £500 million each and every year once fully rolled out. Yet there is currently no Universal Credit, and so savings are having to be found from elsewhere in the budget.

Likewise the new disability benefit, Personal Independence Payment, has taken much longer to roll out than previously intended, turning a proposed saving of £1.2 billion into an overspend of £1.7 billion. While the government's original savings projection took into account the more generous payments that would be made available under Personal Independence Payment to those claimants in greatest need, it had also forecast in the 2012 Budget that there would be 3.2 million disability benefit claimants, including 751,000 on Personal Independence Payment, by 2015-16. Yet the government was forced to concede defeat on this front when the data published alongside the 2015 Budget showed that there would be 3.5 million people claiming disability benefits in 2015-16 – and only 527,000 on Personal Independence Payment – a total of 300,000 wide of the mark.

The government's failure to implement these two major structural reforms necessitated the savings made elsewhere, as we have seen, both to benefit levels and the numbers of people eligible to claim. The Office for Budget Responsibility has found that the largest contributors to the overall fall in welfare expenditure as a proportion of GDP, from 12.8% in 2009-10 to 11.8% in 2014-15, were the reductions in tax credits and Income Support, with fewer people being eligible.[8] There were falls too both in the relative value of these benefits and the number of people claiming out-of-work benefits, while an increase in the number of people receiving Housing Benefit offset a fall in the value of awards.[9]

The government has shown itself able, therefore, to control the working-age welfare budget. But its chosen means of doing so were not explicitly set out in its 2010 programme, nor might they have been quite so necessary had the promised savings been delivered by the rollout of Universal Credit or Personal Independence Payment. In some cases, the policy of compensating for failure elsewhere in the reform programme has come at a great social cost to those claiming the existing range of in- and out-of-work benefits.

## ii. Rebuilding families

There is evidence aplenty of the CSJ's influence on the government's attempts to repair 'broken Britain' in a brief examination of its family policy. Its analysis made clear that no government could ever dream of repairing 'broken Britain' without the help of a fully-fledged Universal Credit and, equally important, repairing the nation's fractured families. Its 2010 programme made clear the government's belief that 'strong and stable families of all kinds are the bedrock of a strong and stable society'.[10]

This was to be achieved by keeping couples together, so that as many children as possible would live with both their birth parents.

An important first move by the government to achieve this crucial objective was to bring all aspects of relationship support into the responsibility of one government department – Iain Duncan Smith's Department for Work and Pensions.

Its 2014 document set out some of the early progress made in achieving 'social justice' through its family policy:[11]

- 250,000 more children are living with both their birth parents.

- The proportion of poor children living with both parents increased from 45% in 2010-11 to 48% in 2011-12.

- Marriage and civil partnerships are to be recognised in the tax system through transferable tax allowances.

- £30 million has been invested to deliver marriage preparation, couple counselling and relationship education.

Important steps and all in the right direction. We applaud the government for recognising, acting upon, and actively promoting this area of policy as a means of nurturing the nation's character through safeguarding the position of children in this way.

Yet more steps might well have been taken had Universal Credit not failed so miserably to deliver on its promise. Whereas Working Tax Credit gives exactly the same level of support to a couple as to a lone parent in otherwise identical circumstances, Universal Credit is designed so that the 'standard allowance' for a couple is worth more than that for a single person with children. In addition, the 'work allowance' – the amount a family can earn before their Universal Credit begins to be withdrawn – is higher for couples than for lone parents. The number of families in 2015 feeling the benefits of this policy remains miniscule.

One step back came in the government's withdrawal of Child Benefit for households in which one earner's income exceeds the higher rate tax threshold. Either lone parents could be put off moving in with a partner or, in some cases, couples might be incentivised to break up.

In the 2015 parliament we suggest the government gives much greater emphasis to stronger families and the role it must play in welfare reform, and to report to parliament and the nation more fully on the details of what will be, hopefully, its continual success.

The government can reflect on some clear signs of progress, but has the overall package been fair between low-income groups and the rest of society, and between working-age benefits – where the cuts have been made – and pensioners who have been afforded the security of the triple lock? These two lines will become increasingly important in the 2015 parliament.

# Conclusion

## An overall audit

Iain Duncan Smith took into government an analysis of 'broken Britain'; the welfare state was seen to be relieving poverty only by entrenching it, and at an ever growing cost to the taxpayer. The major solution was seen to come from introducing Universal Credit. With Universal Credit, so went the analysis, work would always represent the best route out of poverty, dependence on out-of-work benefit would fall, and the cost to the taxpayer of working-age welfare would be brought under control.

Universal Credit was sold to the chancellor of the exchequer and cabinet colleagues as the game changing reform that would fix 'broken Britain'. A second plank of Duncan Smith's programme to cement work as the best route out of poverty has centred on encouraging into work those claimants deemed capable of working, but who previously had been unwilling or unable to get and keep a job. The government's chosen means here have been a single welfare-to-work programme for all long-term benefit claimants and the attachment of strict conditions, enforced by the possible withdrawal of benefit, to the receipt of Jobseeker's Allowance.

An important consideration too in the government's attempts to repair 'broken Britain' is the objective of cutting overall welfare expenditure. Again, its chosen agents were Universal Credit and the welfare-to-work programme. Other tools chosen for this task were the transfer of Incapacity Benefit claimants who were deemed capable of work to Jobseeker's Allowance, and others to a new Employment and Support Allowance, the migration of Disability Living Allowance claimants to a new Personal Independence Payment, reforming eligibility for tax credits, Housing Benefit and support towards Council Tax, and cutting the real value of benefits paid to working-age claimants.

On this latter objective, the government has been successful. It has cut in real terms the size of the working-age welfare budget and, in doing so, it has achieved an objective that had proved elusive even to the Thatcher governments.

What has worked elsewhere amongst the raft of changes to the existing welfare state and the main welfare reform of Universal Credit? We judge the success or otherwise of the government's efforts by assessing their impact on benefit expenditure, the number of people dependent on benefit, and the living standards of those people claiming benefit. Our main criteria of success has been the extent to which each welfare reform contributes to mending 'broken Britain', by helping claimants into work, delivering savings to the taxpayer, and making those households struggling to survive on a low income better off than they were previously.

The task the government set itself in 2010 of achieving all three of these objectives, which together comprise a dysfunctional relationship, has proved not surprisingly difficult to achieve.

# i. Has the government managed to 'Get Britain Working' again?

## *Welfare-to-work*

The government has delivered a reduction in unemployment, proving amongst other things the appropriateness of paying by results those contracted to deliver its single welfare-to-work programme. The Work Programme has been as successful as the previous Labour government's programme in getting claimants into work – 432,000 claimants have found work under the Work Programme – but at half the cost. Moreover the government's system of paying contractors on the basis of their results has made its welfare-to-work programme more successful in a second key area than any of its predecessors. Based on the available data we conclude that those starting a job under the Work Programme are more likely than their counterparts on previous programmes to remain in work for longer periods of time once they have found a job.[1] We judge this as the most important success of the government's welfare-to-work strategy.

The success of this strategy, however, has not been evenly shared. The programme's record for claimants with disabilities is poor. Likewise for those aged over 50.

We believe the payment-by-results system the government introduced now requires a significant recalibration to give the most disadvantaged participants a fighting chance of getting and keeping a job. As the government draws up its new Work and Health Programme – the welfare-to-work policy announced in the 2015 Autumn Statement that will combine the Work Programme and Work Choice – we believe each claimant's strengths and difficulties must be identified as near as possible to the start of a benefit claim, and that the payment-by-results system should be further weighted in favour of claimants deemed to be facing the steepest barriers in their search for work. Those claimants requiring the most intensive support should be referred as early as possible to the Work and Health Programme, and this early referral process should not be limited to claimants of any particular benefit.

We also recommend the government builds on the early success of its voluntary welfare-to-work programme for claimants with disabilities, by gradually lifting the cap in 2016 on the numbers who can enrol on the programme and extending the length of time for which claimants can participate.

### Youth unemployment

The government has delivered a reduction in youth unemployment, although things became much worse before they got better. Had it not so prematurely scrapped the previous Labour government's Future Jobs Fund, the reduction probably would have been even greater. The heavy lifting came in the second half of the last parliament, and has continued into the early part of this one, when an improving economy began creating enough jobs into which some of those young people participating on the main welfare-to-work programme could be placed. The government's Youth Contract, designed by the then Liberal Democrat leader in 2012 specifically to find work for those young people facing the greatest difficulty in doing so, failed compared with the Future Jobs Fund. Further development of the use of the monies put towards the Youth Contract is urgent.

A 'Future Jobs Fund Mark Two' whose business is to create and guarantee jobs for the young unemployed, as did Labour's Future Jobs Fund, could help the government make further inroads into youth unemployment, and all but abolish long-term youth unemployment.

Similarly, the government should explore whether such a model of job creation might enhance the employment prospects of claimants aged 50 and over. The idea again is that they would enrol on a paid work placement before they risk becoming long-term unemployed. Crucially for this group of claimants, Jobcentre Plus should find out as early as possible whether they are equipped with the minimum set of computer literacy skills that are so crucial when seeking and applying for jobs. Those whose skillsets demonstrate a shortfall should be offered immediate help within the job centre, with the objective of such help being to improve these claimants' confidence and abilities on this vital score. Voluntary bodies, mutual and social enterprises should be invited into each job centre to provide this support. Such moves could aid the government in its quest to find further savings from the working-age welfare budget.

## Conditionality

The government has followed Labour in the right direction towards making the receipt of welfare more conditional upon certain duties being met by claimants. Its sanctions policy since 2012 has almost certainly made life in work that much easier than remaining on out-of-work benefit. But this conclusion comes with more than a hint of qualification.

We believe that one of the conditions of drawing benefit must be the duty to seek and prepare for work – conditionality is part of a contract which entails the right to draw benefit being dependent on satisfying one's duty. Yet this principle has now been so applied to an ever greater number of working-age recipients, and with what appears to be such fervency to remove their right to draw benefit, that injustices could well be occurring on a scale unknown; unknown as the government does not collect data, and as a consequence we believe that genuine claimants could be at risk of being exposed to destitution. While around one in five sanctioned claimants appear to have found work following the docking of their benefit money, the government seems unable to account for the remaining four out of five sanctioned claimants.

We recommend, therefore, four urgent reforms to the existing system rather than its abolition. We welcome the government's decision to trial a 'Yellow Card' warning system in place of an immediate financial sanction for those claimants deemed not to have fulfilled their duty of looking for work. Should the Yellow Card fail to prevent injustices from occurring, the government might wish to supplement this policy with the option for Jobcentre Plus staff of issuing a non-financial sanction for a claimant's first failure to meet the terms of their Claimant Commitment.

As a further step, we recommend that the Department for Work and Pensions trials a 'grace period' for vulnerable claimants of Jobseeker's Allowance or Employment and Support Allowance, during which the requirements placed upon them are eased at times of transition or acute difficulty. It might wish to focus this pilot initially on homeless claimants.

As importantly we propose that the government must forthwith begin a survey so that they can answer the simple but crucial question of what happens to the four out of five claimants expelled from the rolls who appear not to find work.

The government is either unwilling or unable to inform us how much expenditure is withdrawn by sanctioning claimants. It should therefore begin to collect these data for obvious reasons.

## ii. Has the government enshrined work as the best route out of poverty?

### *The prevalence of poverty*

The conditionality attached to the receipt of benefit may have made work an easier option, but real wage growth at the bottom end of the labour market has been the missing piece of the government's welfare reform puzzle. While work remains preferable to a life on benefit, bringing with it a significant reduction in the risk of being poor, and the government's efforts have reinforced this outcome, it does not provide complete protection against poverty. The explanation for the government's failure to enshrine work as a failsafe means of guarding against poverty is twofold. First, there have been significant increases both in the extent of low-paid work as well as the number of people moving from low benefit income into low-paid jobs and being parked there; second, cuts have been imposed upon benefits and tax credits claimed by this same group of low-paid workers.

### *The wage scene*

We therefore recommend that the government uses its new National Living Wage to kick-start a national productivity strategy, beginning in low-paying industries, so that it is capable of beginning in the longer run to boost real incomes across the board.

To make this a truly national strategy it should be built upon a new high-speed rail line that links up the great cities of the North, and then works its way down to London.

Low-paid workers should also be given help by Jobcentre Plus to increase their hours and develop their skills, either on the job or after their shift, on courses that in the longer run will boost their output. These moves, we believe, would enhance their chances of gaining higher-paid employment.

Likewise if the government were to signal to employers that they could no longer draw exclusively upon an endless supply of eager workers from eastern Europe, their minds might instead become focused on improving their existing machinery and working practices to get the best out of their labour stock, thereby opening up space for wage increases.

# iii. Has the government delivered 'Welfare That Works'?

## *Universal Credit*

What, then, of Iain Duncan Smith's flagship reform to simplify the benefit system, reduce long-term dependence on welfare and cement work as the best route out of poverty, which sails under the banner of Universal Credit?

It is in the fate of Universal Credit, and the changes that have been made to the original ideas, that we see the collapse of the government's strategy to make work the best route out of poverty. This judgement is not based simply upon the minute number of people claiming Universal Credit – there were barely 75,000 claimants by the 2015 general election when 1.7 million was the goal – and its minimal impact on welfare expenditure. Because of Universal Credit's higher taper rate for many claimants the strategy of fixing 'broken Britain' by offering lower withdrawal rates than the current system lies in ruins. Universal Credit fails to incentivise the work on which the 'broken Britain' analysis was built. If creating an incentive to work is the goal the present system for the vast majority of claimants meets that goal more effectively.

The existing roster of working-age benefits the government inherited remains largely intact, and worse, the marginal tax rates, particularly for tax credits, have been increased. Indeed, the government's reduction in the structural budget deficit has been achieved in part by undermining the cornerstone of its welfare reform strategy of making work pay. The transition from the original design of Universal Credit to the version which began to be rolled out at a glacial pace will reinforce still further the higher marginal tax rates for claimants in low-paid work.

### Tax credits

The government's decision to protect all pensioner benefits has been accompanied by its failure to implement its flagship Universal Credit reform. The benefit savings that were to flow from Universal Credit remain at large. These two developments made it that much more important for the government to implement cuts elsewhere in the working-age welfare budget, in order to make progress on its deficit reduction targets.

A prime target for cuts has been the tax credit bill, which at its peak represented a £30 billion wage subsidy to low-paying employers.

The government has enacted a raft of reforms whose net effect has been to restrict eligibility for tax credits, as well as their generosity. These reforms delivered not insubstantial savings for the taxpayer and helped, to some extent, reduce dependency. But in making the cuts within the existing tax credit system the government, perhaps unintentionally, has hit low-paid workers' living standards. It is nigh on impossible within the current system to limit the entitlements of higher earners without simultaneously clobbering the lowest paid workers. A much more preferable alternative would have been to raise real wages and thereby float people off tax credits. At the very least, the government should have ensured that any changes would affect only new claimants. By cutting existing claimants' entitlements the government has reneged on its side of the contract which guarantees an acceptable minimum to families who do the right thing and go to work.

Thankfully in November 2015 the chancellor called off what looked set to be an all-out blitzkrieg raid on this same group of strivers. He performed a full U-turn on his proposals to reduce the income of 3.2 million low-paid workers in receipt of tax credits by an average of £1,350 in April 2016. In the longer term, though, and given it is here to stay at least for the rest of this parliament, the government must review the whole machinery of the tax credit system. It must aim to be in a position whereby cuts can be made towards the top of the income distribution – those earning, say, twice the level of the new National Living Wage – without necessarily impacting upon those at the very bottom. We set out one potential reform programme in the postscript.

## *Housing Benefit*

Britain's longstanding failure to build enough affordable homes for ownership or rent, coupled with the low wages paid by many of the jobs created since the great recession, has exerted continuous upward pressure on the Housing Benefit bill. This trend has continued since 2010. Despite again introducing a series of reforms to restrict entitlement to, and the generosity of Housing Benefit, the government has overspent on this budget. Aside from the Benefit Cap, none of these reforms seem to have incentivised claimants to seek work.

The longer-term solution to the Housing Benefit crisis is almost too obvious to state. In normal circumstances it would be difficult to meet the existing demand for homes; it becomes incredibly difficult to do so if the government operates an open door immigration policy within the European Union. Our population growth is now being driven almost exclusively by immigration. For a host of reasons, and not simply to meet the housing demand, a future government must control our borders. Now, and at that future date, the obvious answer is relevant, that the only sustainable way to reduce the size of the Housing Benefit budget is to increase the supply of housing by initiating a national housebuilding programme. We propose that a series of skills academies should be established to provide the necessary numbers of bricklayers and other construction workers to sustain such a programme, so that more houses are built without the need to import skilled building workers from abroad, while simultaneously offering skills and jobs to some young people stranded on the welfare rolls. These academies should be delivered by scaling up on a mega scale the work of private training providers who are currently training bricklayers, plasterers, carpenters, roofers, electricians and plumbers in 10 weeks who then begin to work. Each group's first year in work following their 10-week course at a skills academy could be deemed an 'improvement year', in which they are paid at least the National Minimum Wage and are required to hone and perfect the skills they learned at the skills academy. Government-backed inspectors then would award legal certification that brings with it the only genuine prospect of being awarded work in future.

Places with the private providers for the 10-week starter course should be bought on the basis of their known success. Similarly, as bricklayers are unlikely ever to call on the student loans fund, a special fund should be established so that students from working and poorer homes can take out loans to cover the training costs and their living allowance over this short period of time, just as though they were university undergraduates. Wage prospects rise quite quickly for workers trained in this way. Part of this new contract therefore should be the arrangement of repaying loans formed on the model of student finance within, say, two years. Repayment would open the possibility of acquiring other apprenticeship skills at a later date. In this way a whole range of skills can be built up, with one course being the basis on which the next set of skills is built.

## Council Tax

Although not classed as a 'welfare saving', the government cut £471 million from Council Tax Benefit and passed to local authorities the responsibility for delivering the benefit. This move alone sabotaged the chances of Universal Credit achieving its objectives, while also impacting upon the living standards of working-age claimants on low incomes. Many of them are having to pay large sums towards their Council Tax for the first time, thanks, in part, to the government's insistence on exempting all pensioners from the cut. This exemption should become part of a wider public consultation on the justice of continuing a policy that puts all the welfare savings onto working-age claimants.

## iv. Has the government succeeded in reforming incapacity and disability benefits?

### Incapacity Benefit

The government has spent a larger sum on incapacity benefits than that for which it budgeted, as a result of its failed attempts to reduce dependence on this front. The single test determining whether a claimant with disabilities is capable of doing some sort of work proved deeply frustrating, both for claimants and the government. The accumulation of a large backlog of Incapacity Benefit claimants awaiting this test has jarred the government's attempts to find savings in the welfare budget, with the outcomes of the test often disputed by claimants; their grievances centred on the inability of a one-off examination to gauge or consider fully the limiting effects of their health condition. The appeals system found increasingly in the claimant's favour. The government went into the 2015 election having missed by a large margin its targets for reducing expenditure on, and the numbers claiming either Incapacity Benefit or Employment and Support Allowance.

We therefore propose a reform of the single Work Capability Assessment test, so that it becomes a process of learning about each claimant's strengths as against those factors which have limited their efforts to work. An essential part of this process will necessarily involve the integration of health and employment services. The outcome of this would be an 'improving your life' contract which sets out the opportunities that could be opened to claimants, as well as the duties, buttressed by a set of rights and support, that are bestowed upon claimants to support them while they search for some kind of work, ideally linked to a budget to gain the help they need.

For those claimants found capable of some sort of work, however, and who now find themselves on Jobseeker's Allowance, or in the Work Related Activity Group of Employment and Support Allowance, reforms are needed to support them more effectively in their transition into work where this is possible. This will need to tie in, of course, with the 'Welfare Reform Mark Two' that we have outlined. But the welfare contract itself between claimants and the government of the day requires reform so as to ensure claimants' newfound duties in looking for work are properly buttressed with the individual support to find a job. The kind of support that would be most effective should come from undertaking a series of pilots that claimants could help shape.

### Personal Independence Payment

While the government has built on Labour's reforms in the arenas of welfare-to-work, conditionality and Incapacity Benefit, it has trodden new ground in the substitution of Personal Independence Payment for

Disability Living Allowance. This new ground has proven incredibly difficult to negotiate. All of the government's targets for Personal Independence Payment – for claimants to receive greater support, and on savings and numbers claiming – have been missed, while those applying to claim the benefit were often left waiting for months and months and months before finding out whether their claim was successful.

## v. In what areas has the government been most successful?

The government has delivered a drastic reduction in unemployment and worklessness. It has also reinforced the gap between what one could expect to earn in work and receive on benefit. Moreover, where the government has failed to find the savings it had expected from key reforms to incapacity and disability benefits, for example, it gained success many times over with its policy of making life on benefit that much more difficult. The decision to uprate working-age benefits in line with CPI, and then to impose a 1% cap on the uprating of benefit amounts each year, widened overall the gap between what one could expect to earn in work and receive on benefit. This measure yielded ginormous savings but, in doing so, compounded the differential impact of inflation experienced by the poorest households. Not surprisingly, therefore, this policy was forecast to have made 200,000 more children poor.

## vi. Lessons for welfare reformers

The government's welfare reform programme for working-age claimants has produced some real success but also considerable failures. Our hope is that the government will look back to its five-year period in coalition as piloting a series of welfare proposals. It should now build on the most successful initiatives we have highlighted quickly and confidently, while also seeking to fill those gaps we have identified in its reform programme since 2010. It should in particular see the potentially revolutionary impact of George Osborne's National Living Wage strategy. Greater success on the wage front will lessen considerably the significance of its failure on the Universal Credit front. Its most immediate revolutionary impact is to shift welfare reformers' attention away from an exclusive concentration on the Department for Work and Pensions and its programmes to compensate for the dis-welfare of capitalism, to the Department for Business, Innovation and Skills where the responsibility of capitalism to its workforce is being renegotiated. The opening up here of a national productivity strategy, particularly for lower-paying industries, is crucial for two reasons. First, out-of-work benefit claimants, as we have seen, are moved into low-paid employment, and their income needs to be increased in real terms now they are in work. Success on this score would then begin to crack the central economic question of this parliament, namely the productivity conundrum that has engulfed large swathes of the British economy since the great recession. If the new government begins to use its campaign to raise low pay successfully by increasing productivity it would have a strategy to rollout to the rest of the economy. The economic benefits that would flow from this strategy, if shared fairly, would be reaped by everyone in society. Here then lies the third front in welfare reform that the government should open with as much enthusiasm as it can muster.

# Postscript

The government with its National Living Wage is shaking free of the tram lines of the welfare provision of the post-war period. Where might this lead the debate on welfare reform in the next decade?

A key part of the reform agenda will necessarily involve building on the moves taken in the 2010 parliament to strengthen families. Just as the past five years saw progress, albeit tempered, on this front, the Conservatives since the 2015 general election have taken an early step forward before falling off balance. They pledged to enable one member in a married couple or civil partnership to transfer £1,060 of their tax-free income to their partner, where the highest earner is a basic rate taxpayer. A welcome move in itself.

Reformers will need to keep a close eye, though, on another development that is likely to impact upon large numbers of families lower down the income distribution. The two child limit for tax credits might well represent a brand new couple penalty that incentivises large families to split, or lie to the authorities, in order to continue receiving their full entitlement.

And what of the distribution of income between those above and below retirement age? The Conservatives stood in 2015 on the platform of maintaining the protection it had afforded in coalition with the Liberal Democrats to pensioners, but noticeably this was not matched by safeguards against iniquities among the working-age population. A key bone of contention in the run-up to the general election, in fact, was the Tories' failure to outline exactly which groups of the working-age population would bear the greatest brunt of the £12 billion of cuts coming their way between now and 2020.

The chancellor in his 2015 Summer Budget – the first to be delivered by a majority Conservative government since 1996 – revealed with gusto exactly where his axe was to fall. Over a third of the chancellor's cuts – £4.35 billion – were to fall on Britain's 3.2 million lowest paid workers. Voters instinctively ally themselves with this group of strivers, and their loss, on average of £1,350 in April 2016, looked set to send shockwaves through the electorate. Having let down this same group of strivers by failing to deliver on the promises of Universal Credit, the government had stumbled into a blitzkrieg raid on their living standards.

Following an intense cross-party campaign in both Houses of Parliament against this raid, Britain's strivers emerged as the winners from the 2015 Autumn Statement. The chancellor, having declared himself to be in 'listening mode' once the scale of opposition became painfully obvious, performed a full U-turn on these proposed cuts. It was a question of justice that they should win such a concession, although the chancellor has a job on his hands to find the £4.35 billion savings from elsewhere.

Justice also calls for a major survey of what happens to the hundreds of thousands of people thrown off the welfare rolls each year through the sanctioning process. It is unacceptable, not only for this government but for its predecessor and those who will follow, to take away benefit from a mass of people each year and not trouble themselves with how this army of people survive. For that is what is happening under the government's sanctions policy. The ability to track the wellbeing of the whole population is now a part of being a grown up government, let alone a 'One Nation' government.

For those claimants moving into work, we cannot underestimate the importance of the new National Living Wage – the centrepiece of the 2015 Summer Budget. 1.9 million people who currently earn less than £7.20 an hour will receive a direct pay rise in April 2016. This initiative has the potential to revolutionise not only the welfare reform debate, but also the wider economic question of productivity in British industry.

We therefore wish to close this audit by posing a challenge to the government. Welfare Reform Mark One has largely succeeded in moving into work substantial numbers of people previously drawing out-of-work benefit. Welfare Reform Mark Two must widen this route where possible to the least advantaged claimants, namely those with disabilities and those aged over 50.

In order to enshrine work as the best route out of poverty, Welfare Reform Mark Three must build upon the National Living Wage to deliver the higher productivity that can sustain rising real incomes across the board.

Universal Credit alone will not fulfil this task and, judging by the government's constant chipping away at its generosity for lower-paid workers, strivers with children who claim Universal Credit will be worse off next year by up to £2,629.

The prospect of Universal Credit being rolled out in full by the end of this parliament looks increasingly doubtful, and its potential to fix 'broken Britain' has been diminished beyond recognition. We can safely assume from the snail's pace rollout of Universal Credit that tax credits are here to stay at least until 2020.

We therefore hope the chancellor's 'listening mode' on tax credits will continue into 2016, for the whole debate that has arisen on the role of in-work benefits in his much vaunted 'lower tax, lower welfare, higher wage society' has afforded him an opportunity to become a serious welfare reformer. A thorough review of in-work benefits, which looks beyond Universal Credit and takes as its starting point the full protection of lower-paid workers with children, is required.

As a key plank of Welfare Reform Mark Three the chancellor could pause for a year and come up with proposals that, by 2020, will transform the tax credit system as we know it. In doing so he would be sending a clear signal to employers that tax credits will no longer be a means through which low wages are subsidised.

The introduction of the National Living Wage now sets the scene for all welfare reform that will follow under this government. We have set out elsewhere some of the initial steps it might wish to take to boost productivity, and here we outline five tax credit reform proposals that take as the cornerstone a National Living Wage which will reach £9 an hour – £16,000 a year based on a working week of 35 hours – by 2020.

It is tempting to set out reform proposals that assume we are in sight of sunnier uplands after dealing with the structural deficit in the nation's budget. We make a plea not to be beguiled by such a prospect. Our starting point is that the proposed tax credit reforms are within the government's iron envelope of moving Britain to a 'lower tax, lower welfare, higher wage society'. Political earthquakes will be required to shift them from that goal.

By 2020 we suggest as a first reform that childless

couples and single workers without children would no longer be eligible for support from the tax credit system.

A second reform would protect those workers who are vulnerable, with mental illnesses for example, and who could not work a full week at present. They should be able to claim Jobseeker's Allowance or Employment and Support Allowance if they work up to 24 hours a week – going beyond the 16 hours they are allowed to work under the current regime before their claim ceases – adding to that as much part-time work as they are able to command.

The next reform we propose is centring the tax credit system on lower-paid workers with children. We suggest that entitlement should go to families earning up to twice the level of the National Living Wage. In 2020 this would set a ceiling of £32,000. Beyond that point eligibility to tax credits would cease.

The aim of these reforms is not to pull the floor from underneath low earners without children. It is instead to ensure the labour market can provide them with a decent minimum income as well as the prospect of pay progression. A fourth and crucial reform therefore should be to revamp Jobcentre Plus, whose staff should have the skills to help tax credit claimants think about how, over the next four years, they might increase the hours they work in their current job or increase their hours of work and pay by moving to a new job.

To make this reform work, claimants must know they won't lose large chunks of any additional earnings to the taxman. Hence a fifth reform during this four-year transition stage should be to allow tax credit claimants to increase their earnings by up to £5,000 in any 18-month period without any clawback of tax credit entitlement. This move would allow some, maybe many, claimants to increase their earnings before any losses incurred from the tax credit cuts.

These five reforms would be much more effective in protecting those in work on modest earnings than anything the government is proposing. They build around the revolutionary idea the chancellor has introduced into British politics, particularly welfare reform, namely of introducing a National Living Wage. This move begins the process of transferring the responsibility for lower earners' welfare to employers and the Department for Business, Innovation and Skills, and away from the Department for Work and Pensions and Her Majesty's Revenue and Customs. With a National Living Wage the purpose of welfare in compensating for the 'dis-welfare' of the market can become a thing of the past.

Here then are the bones of a welfare-to-work strategy for 2020 and beyond – guaranteeing the prospect of a job for all and enshrining a job as the best route out of poverty, while also delivering savings to the taxpayer and beginning to address the productivity conundrum of the British economy.

Will Universal Credit ever be able to fix 'broken Britain'? Success in our three-pronged welfare-to-work strategy would, for all intents and purposes, make this question redundant. For 'broken Britain' would already have been largely fixed.

# Notes

## Introduction

1  Office for National Statistics, Working and Workless Households, 2014- Statistical Bulletin (2014), p.2.

2  Working Tax Credit is a means-tested supplement designed to top up the wages of low-paid workers to an acceptable minimum. Child Tax Credit is a means-tested supplement designed to top up the incomes of families with children.

3  The National Living Wage is to be introduced in April 2016 at a rate of £7.20 an hour, rising to £9.00 an hour by 2020. The voluntary Living Wage rate in 2015 stood at £9.50 an hour in London, and £7.85 an hour across the rest of the United Kingdom.

4  More than 2 million National Insurance numbers have been issued to eastern European nationals following their accession to an enlarged Europe in 2004. The number of citizens from Poland, Hungary, the Czech Republic, Slovenia, Slovakia, Estonia, Lithuania and Latvia living in this country grew from an estimated 167,000 in 2004 to just over 1 million in 2012. Almost three-quarters of a million eastern Europeans were working here in 2013.

5  The National Minimum Wage currently stands at £6.70 an hour.

## 1. 'Broken Britain': Relieving poverty by entrenching it

1  Centre for Social Justice, 'Breakthrough Britain - Dynamic Benefits: Towards welfare that works' (London: Centre for Social Justice, 2009), p. 14.

2  *Ibid.*

3  Universal Credit is a means-tested benefit which combines Jobseeker's Allowance, Income Support, Employment and Support Allowance, Housing Benefit, and tax credits into one single monthly payment.

4  Written by Frank Field while minister for welfare reform at the Department of Social Security, 'New ambitions for our country: a new contract for welfare' (1998).

5   It is impossible within the current structure to fashion changes which protect the lowest earners while simultaneously taking higher income groups out of Working Tax Credit.

6   Ten MPs, two peers and a special adviser were party to negotiations: David Laws, Danny Alexander, Chris Huhne, Andrew Stunnell, Lord Mandelson, William Hague, Oliver Letwin, George Osborne, Ed Llewellyn, Lord Adonis, Harriet Harman, Ed Balls and Ed Miliband.

7   HM Government, 'The Coalition: our programme for government' (London: Cabinet Office, 2010), p. 23.

8   Accessed via http://www.politicsresources.net/area/uk/man/lab97.htm

## 2. Has the government managed to 'Get Britain Working' again?

1   National Audit Office, 'The Work Programme' (London: National Audit Office, July 2014), p.24.

2   Centre for Economic and Social Inclusion, 'DWP Work Programme: how is it performing?' (March 2015), available at: http://cesi.org.uk/responses/dwp-work-programme-how-it-performing-4

3   Pathways To Work was mandatory only for new claimants of Incapacity Benefit.

4   Department for Work and Pensions, 'New Deal for Disabled People: Third synthesis report – key findings from the evaluation' (London: HM Stationery Office, 2007), p.1.

5   Edward Beale, 'Employment and Training Programmes for the Unemployed' (London: House of Commons Library, 2005), p.71.

6   Department for Work and Pensions, 'New Deal for Disabled People: Third synthesis report – key findings from the evaluation' (London: HM Stationery Office, 2007), p.3.

7   Anne Corden and Katherine Nice, 'Pathways to Work: Findings from the final cohort in a qualitative longitudinal panel of incapacity benefit recipients' (London: Department for Work and Pensions, 2006), p.7.

8   Ibid.

9   Department for Work and Pensions, 'Work Programme Evaluation: the participant experience report' (December 2014), available                                                                at: http://www.york.ac.uk/inst/spru/pubs/pdf/rrep892.pdf, p.79.

10  Department for Work and Pensions, 'Work Choice: Official Statistics – May 2015', p.11.

11   This cap was set at six months.

12   http://tabulation-tool.dwp.gov.uk/new_deals/nd50plus/live/
n50_j_i/i_jobyear/e_jcreg/a_stock_r_i_jobyear_c_e_jcreg_aug11.
html

13   Department for Work and Pensions, 'Work Programme
Evaluation: Operation of the commissioning model, finance and
programme delivery – Research report 893' (December 2014), pp.
143-144.

14   National Audit Office, (London: National Audit Office, July 2014),
p.23.

15   National Audit Office, 'The Work Programme' (London: National
Audit Office, July 2014), p.51.

16   Written evidence from the Centre for Economic and Social
Inclusion and NIACE (WTW0041), 7 September 2015, available
here:
http://data.parliament.uk/writtenevidence/committeeevidence
.svc/evidencedocument/work-and-pensions-
committee/welfare-to-work/written/20087.pdf

17   The Conservative Party, 'Invitation to Join the Government of
Great Britain: The Conservative Manifesto 2010', p.15.

18   National Audit Office, 'The New Deal for Young People' (London:
HM Stationery Office, January 2002).

19   Alistair Darling's programme drew on the efforts to find work
prior to World War One. This approach was swept away with
Lloyd George's unemployment insurance scheme.

20   Office for National Statistics, various editions of 'Labour Market
Statistics'.

21   DWP, 'Impacts and Costs and Benefits of the Future Jobs Fund'
(2012).

22   House of Commons Committee of Public Accounts, '16- to 18-
year-old participation in education and training' (HM Stationery
Office, January 2015): p.9.

23   There is no definite source of data with which to make direct
comparisons.

## 3.   Swinging the pendulum of conditionality: making work the easier option

1   Deacon, A.J. (2002) Perspectives on welfare: ideas, ideologies and
policy debates. Open University Press.

2   Deacon, A.J. (2002) Perspectives on welfare: ideas, ideologies and
policy debates. Open University Press.

3 Real global GDP grew at 5.5% in the decade to 1971, 3.7% in the decade to 1981, 3.1% in the decade to 1991 and again to 2001, and 3.9% in the decade to 2011, according to World Economics: http://www.worldeconomics.com/papers/Global%20Growth%20Monitor_7c66ffca-ff86-4e4c-979d-7c5d7a22ef21.paper

4 For a summary of the conditionality debate in the post-war period see Beyond Punishment by Frank Field and Matthew Owen, Institute of Community Studies, 1994.

5 See, for example, Church Action on Poverty, the Baptist Union of Great Britain, the United Reformed Church, the Methodist Church, the Church of Scotland, and the Church of Wales, 'Time to rethink benefit sanctions', available here: http://www.methodist.org.uk/news-and-events/news-releases/new-data-more-than-100-people-per-day-with-mental-health-problems-are-having-their-benefits-sanctioned

6 See, for example, Andrew Forsey, 'An Evidence Review for the All-Party Parliamentary Inquiry into Hunger in the United Kingdom' (London: The Children's Society, 2014): p.61.

7 Ibid.

8 Detailed statistics on the number of individuals sanctioned between October 2012 and March 2015 are available on the Department for Work and Pensions' Stat-Xplore website.

9 https://sw.stat-xplore.dwp.gov.uk/webapi/jsf/tableView/tableView.xhtml#

10 https://www.gov.uk/government/statistics/jobseekers-allowance-and-employment-and-support-allowance-sanctions-decisions-made-to-march-2015

11 House of Commons Work and Pensions Committee, 'Oral evidence: Benefit sanctions policy beyond the Oakley Review', HC 814, (2015): http://data.parliament.uk/writtenevidence/committeeevidence.svc/evidencedocument/work-and-pensions-committee/benefit-sanctions-policy-beyond-the-oakley-review/oral/17970.pdf

12 Paul Gregg, 'Realising Potential: A Vision for Personalised Conditionality and Support', DWP (2008)

13 Andrew Forsey, 'An Evidence Review for the All-Party Parliamentary Inquiry into Hunger in the United Kingdom' (London: The Children's Society, 2014): p.59.

14 Rachel Loopstra et al, 'Do punitive approaches to unemployment benefit recipients increase welfare exit and employment? A cross-area analysis of UK sanctioning reforms', University of Oxford, Sociology Work Paper 2015-1 (January 2015).

15  Centre for Social Justice, 'Up to the job? How reforming Jobcentre Plus will help tackle worklessness' (London: Centre for Social Justice, 2013) p.4.

16  Dr Alex Nunn and Dr Dave Devins, 'Process evaluation of the Jobcentre Plus Performance Management Framework' (London: Department for Work and Pensions, 2012), p.21.

17  *Ibid*, p.30.

18  *Ibid*, p.30.

19  An analysis conducted by the House of Commons Library of the Labour Force Survey shows that at least 5.6 million workless individuals of working age out of a total of 10.9 million claim benefit. Nobody knows the circumstances of the remaining 5.3 million fellow citizens. Many may be fine and living on an income independent of work or welfare. But what of the rest?

20  House of Commons Library calculations.

## 4. Raising the bar to making work pay

1  Reformers present at Speenhamland's Pelican Inn just before the turn of the 19th century developed a system of ratepayer-funded subsidies with which local authorities could supplement low wages. This system was soon to become the only welfare reform show in town, in respect of providing workers with a more acceptable minimum than their wages would afford them and their families.

2  Andrew Hood and David Phillips, 'Benefit Spending and Reforms: The Coalition Government's Record' (Institute for Fiscal Studies, January 2015).

3  Benefit caseload and expenditure tables published alongside Budget 2015, available at: https://www.gov.uk/government/statistics/benefit-expenditure-and-caseload-tables-2015

4  Office for Budget Responsibility, 'Welfare trends report' (OBR, October 2014): p.5.

5  House of Commons Library analysis of the Office for National Statistics' 'Family Spending' surveys. Net rent refers to rent that is net of Housing Benefit.

6  Office for Budget Responsibility,'Welfare trends report October 2014', p.43.

7  This includes Universal Credit claimants as well as those households claiming existing legacy benefits. The data is available at: https://www.gov.uk/government/uploads/system/uploads/attachment_data/file/426846/benefit-cap-statistics-to-feb-2015.pdf

8   The Troubled Families programme was set up by the Coalition to 'turn around' the lives of 120,000 families in England who are workless and deemed most likely to succumb to truancy and antisocial behaviour.

9   'Impact Assessment – Housing Benefit: Changes to the Local Housing Allowance Arrangements' (November 2010).

10  Department for Work and Pensions, 'The impact of recent reforms to Local Housing Allowances: Summary of key findings' (London: DWP, July 2014).

11  Department for Work and Pensions, 'The impact of recent reforms to Local Housing Allowances: Summary of key findings' (London: DWP, July 2014).

12  Department for Work and Pensions, 'Impact Assessment-Housing Benefit: Under occupation of social housing' (June 2012): https://www.gov.uk/government/uploads/system/uploads/at tachment_data/file/214329/social-sector-housing-under-occupation-wr2011-ia.pdf

13  http://www.newstatesman.com/politics/2014/03/esther-mcvey-flounders-bedroom-tax-failure-becomes-clear

14  Department for Work and Pensions, 'Evaluation of Removal of the Spare Room Subsidy, Interim Report' (London: DWP, July 2014).

15  Ipsos MORI, 'One year on: The impact of welfare reforms on housing association tenants' (May 2014), available at https://www.ipsos-mori.com/Assets/Docs/Publications/NHF-Phase2_Tenant-Survey-Report_19.05.14.pdf

16  Ibid.

17  The Institute for Fiscal Studies estimates that rents fell by only 10% of these cuts: http://www.ifs.org.uk/uploads/publications/conferences/presentations/PRES0515RJ050315.pdf

18  Local Government Association, 'Skills to build: Creating the houses and jobs our communities need' (August 2015).

19  Sam Ashton, Marc Francis and Megan Jarvie, 'Too poor to pay: the impact of the second year of localised Council Tax support in London' (London: Child Poverty Action Group and Zacchareus 2000, 2015).

20  StepChange Debt Charity, 'Council tax debts: How to deal with the growing arrears crisis tipping families into problem debt' (2015), available at: https://www.stepchange.org/Portals/0/documents/media/reports/Council-tax-debt-report-2015.pdf

21  Department for Communities and Local Government, 'Local Government Finance Bill: Localising support for council tax' (June 2012), available at: https://www.gov.uk/government/

uploads/system/uploads/attachment_data/file/8465/2158675.pdf

## 5. Work as the best route out of poverty?

1   Lorna Adams *et al*, 'Destinations of Jobseeker's Allowance, Income Support and Employment and Support Allowance Leavers 2011' (London: Department for Work and Pensions, 2012).

2   Mike Brewer, David Phillips, and Luke Sibieta, 'Living Standards, Inequality and Poverty: Labour's Record' (London: Institute for Fiscal Studies, 2010): p.22.

3   Measured in relative terms After Housing Costs, in Table 5a, Estimated percentage of working-age adults in relative/absolute low income , United Kingdom, 'Households below average income: 1994/1995 to 2013/2014'.

4   James Browne and William Elming, 'The effect of the coalition's tax and benefit changes on household incomes and work incentives' (London: Institute for Fiscal Studies, 2015): p.18.

5   Office for National Statistics, 'Working and Workless Households, 2014 – Statistical Bulletin', available at http://www.ons.gov.uk/ons/dcp171778_382704.pdf

6   Measured After Housing Costs in 'Households Below Average Income 1994-95 to 2013-14', Table 5.7db.

7   Stuart Adam and James Browne, 'Do the UK Government's welfare reforms make work pay?' (London: Institute for Fiscal Studies, 2013), p.1.

8   Measured After Housing Costs in 'Households Below Average Income 1994-95 to 2009-10', Table 5.4db, and in 'Households Below Average Income 1994-95 to 2013-14', Table 5.4db.

9   James Browne and William Elming, 'The effects of the coalition's tax and benefit changes on household incomes and work incentives' (London: Institute for Fiscal Studies, 2015): p.19.1

10  *Ibid*, p.25.

11  'Under-employment won't return to pre-crisis levels until 2023, says TUC', January 2015, https://www.tuc.org.uk/economic-issues/labour-market/britain-needs-pay-rise/under-employment-won%E2%80%99t-return-pre-crisis-levels

12  Alex Hurrell, *Starting out or getting stuck? An analysis of who gets trapped in low paid work – and who escapes* (November 2013), available at: http://www.resolutionfoundation.org/wp-content/uploads/2014/08/Starting-out-or-getting-stuck-FINAL.pdf

13  http://www.ft.com/cms/s/0/7a70828e-b36b-11e3-bc21-
00144feabdc0.html#axzz3QyW3vaFT

14  Office for National Statistics, 'Self-employed workers in the UK
– 2014', p.7: http://www.ons.gov.uk/ons/dcp171776_374941.pdf

15  Office for Budget Responsibility, 'Welfare trends report' (OBR,
October 2014): p.40.

## 6.  Universal Credit: 'Welfare That Works'?

1  This rate, which to most claimants feels like an effective tax rate,
is applied to post-tax earnings and comprises the loss of out-of-
work benefits.

2  https://www.gov.uk/government/uploads/system/uploads
/attachment_data/file/220177/universal-credit-wr2011-ia.pdf

3  Mike Brewer, James Brown, and Wenchao Jin, 'Universal Credit:
A preliminary analysis' (London: Institute for Fiscal Studies,
2011).

4  David Finch, Making the most of UC: *Final report of the Resolution
Foundation review of Universal Credit* (June 2015), available at:
http://www.resolutionfoundation.org/wp-
content/uploads/2015/06/UC-FINAL-REPORT1.pdf

5  Brent, Doncaster, Harrow, North Kesteven, and Trafford have
each set a Council Tax support withdrawal rate of 30%.
Brentwood, Mid Sussex and Wiltshire have each set a rate of 15%.

6  Department for Work and Pensions, 'Universal Credit: welfare
that works' (Department for Work and Pensions, November
2010), p.37.

7  Office for Budget Responsibility, 'Welfare trends report' (London:
HM Stationery Office, June 2015) .

8  Office for Budget Responsibility, 'Welfare trends report' (London:
HM Stationery Office, October 2014).

9  http://www.independent.co.uk/news/uk/politics/exclusive-
we-know-tax-credits-were-overpaid-now-its-revealed-the-figure-
is-56bn-9701865.html

10  Paul Treloar, 'Is Universal Credit working' in *Child Poverty Action
Group Welfare Rights Bulletin 243* (December 2014).

11  See, for example, Department for Work and Pensions, 'Universal
Credit: welfare that works' (November 2010).

12  David Finch, Adam Corlett, and Vidhya Alakeson, 'Universal
Credit: A policy under review' (London: Resolution Foundation,
August 2014).

## 7. Dividing the sheep and the goats?

1   The phrase one doctor used to describe his actions when charged with killing his elderly patients, in Patrick Devlin, *Easing the passing: The Trial of Doctor John Bodkin Adams* (The Bodley Head, 1985).

2   Explanatory Memorandum to the Employment and Support Allowance (Transitional Provisions, Housing Benefit and Council Tax Benefit) (Existing Awards) Regulations 2010: http://www.legislation.gov.uk/uksi/2010/875/pdfs/uksiem_20100875_en.pdf

3   Office for Budget Responsibility, 'Welfare trends report – June 2015' (London: HM Stationery Office, 2015).

4   BBC News, 'Hundreds of thousands hit by benefits backlog', http://www.bbc.co.uk/news/uk-27796739

5   https://www.gov.uk/government/uploads/system/uploads/attachment_data/file/434838/pip-stats-apr-2013-apr-2015.pdf

6   http://cdn.budgetresponsibility.independent.gov.uk/49754-OBR-Welfare-Accessible-v0.2.pdf

7   Office for Budget Responsibility, 'Welfare trends report – October 2014', p.113.

8   https://www.gov.uk/government/uploads/system/uploads/attachment_data/file/220176/dla-reform-wr2011-ia.pdf

9   https://www.gov.uk/government/statistics/benefit-expenditure-and-caseload-tables-2015

## 8. Big successes

1   Andrew Hood and David Phillips, 'Benefit Spending and Reforms: The Coalition Government's Record' (London: Institute for Fiscal Studies, January 2015).

2   Andrew Hood and David Phillips, 'Benefit Spending and Reforms: The Coalition Government's Record' (London: Institute for Fiscal Studies, 2015)

3   Office for National Statistics, 'National Population Projections, 2012-based Statistical Bulletin' (November 2013), p.5.

4   Andrew Hood and David Phillips, 'Benefit Spending and Reforms: The Coalition Government's Record' (London: Institute for Fiscal Studies, 2015), p.6.

5   http://www.telegraph.co.uk/finance/personalfinance/pensions/11430359/Pensioners-are-now-richer-than-the-rest-and-we-should-celebrate-that.html

6    The Secretary of State for Work and Pensions in May 2014 stated in correspondence to Frank Field that 'not introducing time-limiting would cost around £1bn in 14/15'.

7    The Library examined benefit expenditure as forecast at the 2010 Autumn Statement, compared with how it stood at the 2015 Budget.

8    Office for Budget Responsibility, 'Welfare Trends Report – October 2014'.

9    Ruth Lupton *et al*, 'The Coalition's Social Policy Record: Policy, Spending and Outcomes 2010-2015', p.23.

10   HM Government, 'The Coalition: our programme for government' (London: Cabinet Office, 2010), p.19.

11   HM Government, 'Social justice: transforming lives – progress report' (London, Department for Work and Pensions, November 2014).

## Conclusion: An overall audit

1    To be fair the Labour government did not attempt to measure the numbers in work for longer than three months.